Morris Rosenthal

Build Your Own PC

second edition

MCGRAW-HILL
Professional Book Division

New York / St. Louis / San Francisco / Auckland / Bogotá / Caracas
Lisbon / London / Madrid Mexico City / Milan / Montreal / New Delhi
San Juan / Singapore / Sydney / Tokyo / Toronto

McGraw-Hill

A Division of The McGraw-Hill Companies

Copyright © 2000 by The McGraw-Hill Companies, Inc. All rights reserved. Printed in the United States of America. Except as permitted under the United States Copyright Act of 1976, no part of this publication may be reproduced or distributed in any form or by any means, or stored in a data base or retrieval system, without the prior written permission of the publisher.

2 3 4 5 6 7 8 9 0   PBT/PBT   0 5 4 3 2 1 0

ISBN 0-07-212467-9

The sponsoring editor for this book was Michael Sprague and the production manager was Clare Stanley. It was set in Melior by Patricia Wallenburg.

Printed and bound by Phoenix Book Technology.

contents

list of figures

Any book written on the subject of building new PCs is aimed at a moving target. After all, a major new generation of PCs appears every other year, and new performance levels for components are attained every few months. However, the underlying standards to which PCs are built change very slowly, and a new winner has only recently emerged—ATX (AT eXtension). Just as the original AT standard ruled the roost for over a decade beginning in 1985, the new ATX standard will carry us well into the opening years of the twenty-first century. In this book, we will build four standard ATX systems with step-by-step illustrated instructions. Each system will be representative of a different family of technology under the ATX umbrella, and the majority of the components used can be mixed and matched amongst these four systems to create a dazzling range of styles, capabilities, and price points. The speeds and capacities of the components you purchase may exceed those of some of the components available when this book went to press, but you can be sure that the basic procedures will remain the same. This second edition of *Build Your Own PC* has been updated and expanded to include the latest technologies, especially Pentium III and Athlon processors.

One of the hardest decisions for the author of a PC book is whether or not to include pricing information, which changes faster than ink dries. Our approach is to include price ranges for all the components used, from basic parts that will result in a complete PC with a price tag under $500 to high-performance parts that will add up to a system costing $2,500 or more. Just remember that PCs are tools with a relatively short lifetime, not an investment. You can still use your grandfather's wood-handled hammer to drive a nail, but with computers, this is not the case. The software programmers that produce the "nails" your computer will use are always rewriting that software to take advantage of the newest features included in the "hammer," and in a few short years, whatever PC you build will be unable to run the latest software without a major upgrade.

The hardest decision for the user of a computer-building book is deciding how much to spend on parts. Once you've picked a dollar amount, the rest is easy. With the help of this book, you can select the best combination of parts to fit your budget. However, until you make the dollars decision, shopping will be a nightmare. For any component you consider, there will be a faster one, or a higher-capacity unit, available for just another $20 or $50. The next performance level can be reached for $75 or $100 and so on, until you reach the latest and greatest component in every category and exceed the limit on your credit card. Then, three months later while surfing the Web, you'll see an ad for a PC with exactly the same components as yours, and it will already cost $500 less than the one you put together. Don't spend more now in the hopes of keeping up with the future. Wait for the future and upgrade. Once you've built your own PC, you will see how easily and cost-effectively you can upgrade it when the need arises.

CHAPTER 1

First Time Builders

This chapter is written for first-time PC builders, who may also have limited experience with the parts and vocabulary of computers. All of the PCs we will build in this book are the new-style ATX (AT eXtension), but we will occasionally refer to the original AT standard to illustrate changes and improvements. Feel free to skim or skip anything that you're already comfortable with, moving on to parts selection and the step-by-step assembly guide. However, even if you've been using a PC longer than a microwave oven, you may find that you've been taking it for granted. After all, how many people know that the microwave utilizes a 2.2-GHz (gigahertz) magnetron tube to heat the food, or why?

Speaking of gigahertz, now is as good a time as any to get the most basic part of PC vocabulary out of the way: the units of measure. Almost all PC components will have one or more units attached to them to describe storage capacity (bytes), speed (hertz, seconds), transfer rate (bits or bytes per second), power consumption (watts), and visual properties (dots per inch, dot size). Most of these units are expressed in quantities of millions, billions, and trillions, or as the reciprocal fractions (millionths, billionths, trillionths). The truth is, you don't really need to remember the real value of these units to make informed decisions; it's only their relative weight that matters. Thus, a 16.4-GB (gigabyte) hard drive has twice as much storage capacity as an 8.2-GB hard drive. Both drives store billions of bytes (1 GB = 1 billion bytes), but you don't need to worry about the value of a billion or the meaning of a byte to pick a hard drive off the shelf. Just for the record, a byte can store a numerical value between 0 and 255, which can be interpreted as a letter or symbol according to a standard code. The most important figure of merit for all computer parts is measured in the tens or hundreds—of dollars. Rather than presenting all of the units associated with computer parts at this point and expecting you to memorize them, we'll simply explain the units each time they are encountered and include a table at the end of the chapter for reference.

The basic parts in a computer are dependent on each other to carry out their functions. For example, all of the parts depend on the power supply for electrical current at the correct voltage levels for operation, and some parts, such as the CPU and memory, are dependent on the motherboard to further refine the power for them. This makes it very difficult to explain the functions of these parts without referring to others, so we will try to tackle them in an order that minimizes the confusion. All in all, there are somewhere between 10 and 15 distinct parts in the average PC, including the monitor, keyboard, and mouse. By distinct parts, we mean parts that you pick off a store shelf or order out of a catalog. Assembling all of these parts to make a working PC will require you to make about 10 push-together connections and screw in around 30 screws (4 in this, 6 in that—nothing complicated).

Case and Power Supply

The case, or system box, is almost universally sold with the power supply included in the price and installed, so we treat case and power supply as a single part. You can build a computer on a workbench without a case (technicians often do this when testing parts), but it takes up a lot of space, interferes with the radio, and is awfully hard to pick up and move in one trip. The function of the case is to house all of the parts that make up your computer, provide ventilation for the heat they produce, and protect the local environment from radio frequency interference. All electrical devices that produce radio frequency emissions are required by law to be certified by the Federal Communications Commission (FCC) as noninterfering with assigned broadcast frequencies. Computers produce lots of radio frequency "noise" in the FM radio band and higher, but at very low power levels. Normally, if a computer in your home interferes with a radio or television, moving it to another room, or even changing its location in the room, will fix the problem. Computer parts are sold as being FCC Class A or B approved, where Class A rating is for business use and Class B rating meets more stringent limits for residential use. Assembling a collection of approved parts is no guarantee that the completed computer would pass an FCC test suite for one rating or the other, but as a home hobbyist, you aren't required to have your computer tested. However, if you decide you love building PCs so much that you want to go into business selling thousands of them, you'll want to buy partially assembled or packaged systems that come with an FCC approval sticker.

The power supply, which is normally sold as part of the case assembly, has two basic functions. The primary function is to supply electrical current to the parts in the computer at the proper, regulated voltage levels. Computer parts require a variety of direct current (DC) voltages, none of which exceeds 12 volts, but the power supply itself operates on 115 volts alter-

Figure 1.1

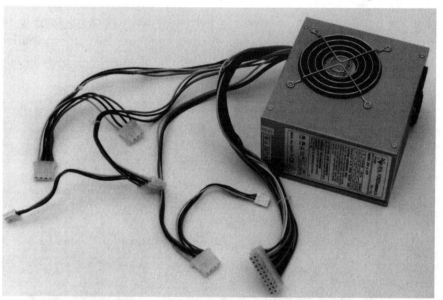

ATX power supply.

nating current (VAC) from the wall socket, so you never want to remove the sealed cover of the supply or stick your screwdriver in through the fan grille. Power supplies can be manually switched to operate on a 230-VAC connection, for Europe and most other regions of the world that do not use the U.S. standard 115-VAC distribution system. On older computer systems (AT standard), the 115 VAC was wired to a switch on the front of the system box, just like the switch for a lamp or a toaster oven. In our new-style PCs (ATX standard), this 115 VAC never leaves the power supply. The power supply in a new computer is never entirely "off," unless it is unplugged or equipped with an external switch on the rear. Instead, it is always supplying a small current to the motherboard, which can tell the power supply when to "wake up" fully, such as when the phone connected to the modem rings or when you press the low-voltage power switch (really a logic switch) on the front of the case.

The second function of the power supply is to cool itself and the parts in the case by use of a fan contained in the power supply. ATX motherboards are designed to put the components with the greatest need for cooling directly in the path of this cool airflow generated by the power supply. Even with this advanced design, some manufacturers recommend that an additional case fan be used with their products. When the power supply and the system are put in their power-saving "sleep" mode, the fan is also automatically turned off, since the amount of heat generated is now minimal.

Motherboard

The motherboard, or mainboard, is normally the first component to be installed in the case. All additional adapters and modules will be installed directly on the motherboard, and drives will be attached to it by wide rib-

Figure 1.2

ATX motherboard Socket 370 CPU installed.

bon cables. However, systems are rarely described by their motherboard, but rather by their central processing unit (CPU), which is our next topic. Some components that are installed on the motherboard, such as the Athlon, Pentium III, or other type of CPU, and the memory (RAM), require no connection to anything else in the case other than the motherboard and can therefore be secured on the motherboard before the motherboard is installed in the case. Not surprisingly, the motherboard is the largest component you will install in the case, but it usually rates about third for cost, after the CPU and hard drive.

The modern ATX motherboard provides many basic functions. It passes power from the power supply to the installed adapters and modules; provides connection ports for the keyboard, mouse, and printer; and integrates all of the supporting functions necessary to make the CPU into a computer. Most of the jobs handled by the motherboard go on entirely in the background, transparent to the user and remarked on only if there is a problem. The main function of the motherboard that you should have in mind when building your PC is that it acts as the communications infrastructure for the entire computer. The motherboard is crisscrossed by information superhighways, some as wide as 64 lanes, which move information and instructions from one component to another.

For example, to display a checkbook ledger stored on your system last week, the CPU (which does most of the decision making) asks the hard drive, via a motherboard superhighway, to send this information to immediate memory for use. The information requested is moved from the hard drive to memory (RAM) via a motherboard superhighway, where the CPU operates on it via a special expressway to memory and formats it for presentation. The formatted checkbook register is then sent, via another superhighway, to the video adapter, which translates it into television-type signals and sends it to the monitor for display. You don't have to keep track of which superhighway, called a *bus*, is involved in every operation, but it's important to understand that the various push-together connections you will make to the motherboard form vital bridges for the information flow.

The most common reason for a part in a new computer not to work is a bad connection at the motherboard. This can be a connection that isn't fully made or a cable attached backward or off-center. Making these connections only takes a few seconds, so remember to look twice before pushing things together, and expect to see this warning repeated in the assembly instructions. Also, since ATX motherboards are always "on," the power supply should be unplugged before adding RAM, before inserting adapters, and before doing any work that may lead to a screw getting away and rolling around under the motherboard until it finds the one place it can cause a short circuit. The newest power supplies are equipped with a small override switch on the back of the supply that can be turned off before you work on the system, in lieu of unplugging the power cord.

Central Processing Unit (CPU)

The CPU is the brain of your PC, which executes and controls the flow of the software programs you run, such as Windows 2000, Linux, Word, or Quicken. The speed of the CPU is often the biggest factor in the overall performance of your PC, which is why most PCs are named by their CPU and speed. Currently, all of the CPUs being manufactured for use in PCs run in the range of 400 to 1000 megahertz (MHz), where MHz expresses the number of steps, in millions, that the CPU can execute in one second. This means that today's CPUs are running between 400 million and 1 billion operations per second. If you should ask "What can a CPU do in a single step?", the answer is "It depends on the CPU." Some CPUs can do two things at once. Others can do six or seven. It depends on the particular design. To keep things reasonable for the consumer, the MHz rating of Intel and AMD CPUs can be assumed as equivalent measures. It's not an exact measure, because it depends in part on what kind of task the PC is working on, but it's a good enough comparison for shopping purposes.

The CPU has a small amount of superfast built-in memory, called *internal cache*. Depending on the type of work the CPU is doing, it may find as much as 90 percent of the information it wants in this internal cache. This is supplemented by another level of extra-fast memory called L2 (level 2), or *external cache*. The recent slot package CPUs, like the Athlon for slot A and Pentium III for Slot 1, include the L2 cache in the CPU package. Socket 7 CPUs, like the AMD K6 series, utilize L2 cache built onto the

Figure 1.3

AMD Athlon.

motherboard. The latest Socket 370 CPUs from Intel, including inexpensive versions of the Pentium III and Celeron, integrate a smaller amount of L2 cache directly on the chip. In all cases, L2 cache is relatively expensive and is normally limited to somewhere between a minimum of 128 KB (on chip) to a maximum 2 MB (on the motherboard or in the slot-type cartridge). This usually amounts to 3 percent or less of the total memory present in the system.

System Memory or RAM

Random Access Memory (RAM) provides the fast, temporary storage from which your CPU draws the information it needs to execute a program. The temporary storage capacity of RAM is measured in megabytes (millions of bytes). You'll want to build your PC with an absolute minimum of 32 MB of RAM. People who run very demanding applications may install 256 MB or more, but for the average user, 64 MB is an excellent compromise figure. Salespeople and magazine articles make a lot of hay out of the different memory technologies and speeds, but the latest commercial innovation, RAMBUS, is tremendously expensive and is only used in a limited

Figure 1.4

Pair of 128-MB PC-100 memory modules.

number of business workhorses. For the best overall price/performance, purchase the largest quantity of memory suitable to your motherboard that fits your PC budget, as opposed to smaller amounts of higher-performance RAM. Memory, amusingly enough, forgets everything the moment the PC is turned off, which is why we have hard drives, CDs, and floppies to provide permanent storage. The fastest way to tip off a showroom vulture that you are a little hazy about computer terminology is to refer to the "memory in the hard drive."

Floppy Drives

Floppy drives have been around almost as long as the reel-to-reel tape drives that played such a big role in 1960s movies, where the reels spinning back and forth showed that the computer was "thinking." The floppy drive used in the vast majority of today's PCs is the 1.44-MB (that's about a million and a half bytes of capacity) or the 3.5-inch floppy. Floppy drives once played a critical part in getting a new PC up and running, but this role has been replaced by bootable CDs. The primary use of floppy disks today is for transporting small files between stand-alone PCs or to make a copies of files for safekeeping. Floppy disks cost pennies and can be carried in a shirt pocket or purse, but there are a couple downsides to using them. Exchange of "infected" floppies may still be the most common way of transmitting computer viruses, and they can lose their data if exposed to a strong magnetic field or left on the shelf too many years. Even worse, because the drives are so cheap yet contain so many mechanical parts that can go out of alignment, the disks written (recorded) in one drive may not work in another! The major role floppy disks once played in software distribution has been replaced by CD-ROM and network downloads.

Figure 1.5

A 1.44-MB floppy drive.

Hard Drives

The most important storage device in your PC is the hard drive. A hard drive can store several thousand times as much information as a floppy drive, and it can find and read that information more quickly than any other storage device, including CD-ROM, DVD-ROM, and tape and floppy drives. The majority of the storage space on your hard drive is used for storing programs, such as the Windows operating system, your Internet software, word processor, golf game, and checkbook. To fill up a standard hard drive with your own words, you would have to write thousands of full-length novels. However, if you record CD-quality music on your hard drive, 20 or 30 hours worth will fill it up! Hard drives have become very reliable, normally outlasting the useful lifetime of the computer in which they are installed. Although you can make room on a full disk by destroying (deleting) old programs or information, most people prefer to let the clutter build up like old boxes in the attic, simply adding another hard disk if it gets too crowded.

Figure 1.6

Western Digital Caviar hard drive.

The storage provided by the hard drive is certainly permanent in comparison to RAM, but anybody using a PC for more than games or surfing the Net should get in the habit of making copies of important information, a process known as "creating a backup." Creating a backup can be as simple as copying your checkbook register or word-processing documents onto a floppy disk once a week. In fact, providing for small backups is the primary function of floppy drives in today's PCs. You should never use floppy disks to exclusively store documents in place of the hard drive, because they are actually less reliable, not to mention much slower. In critical business applications, a special technology called *RAID* (Redundant Array of Inexpensive Drives) provides a means to duplicate data across several individual hard drives to protect against catastrophic failure. RAID solutions often provide automatic failover, so you won't experience any lost time if a drive fails in the middle of the business day. Tape backups remain critical to protect against fire, theft, data management errors, or intentional destruction of data, because the tapes can be stored in a remote location. CD recorders (CDRs) also provide an excellent option for data backup, particularly for archival purposes. Cartridge drives from Iomega and SyQuest, and Imation's 120-MB SuperDrive floppy drive are also options for the home user.

CD-ROM Drives

CD-ROM discs, generally called CDs, were first developed by the music industry to compete with, then replace, vinyl records. The CD drives in PCs are all capable of playing music CDs without the aid of any other hardware, and most come with a headphone jack on the front of the drive. A CD holds a 3-mile-long spiral of information, where the location of any particular item is measured in minutes and seconds from the beginning, as if it were being played in a stereo. The speed at which a stereo plays a CD, or at which your computer CD drive runs when playing music CDs, is

F i g u r e   1 . 7

44X CD-ROM drive.

known as *single speed*, or *1X*. The standard CD drive in use today can read software CDs at peak speeds up to 44X or faster.

CD Recorders

For less than $200, you can purchase a CDR drive that can also record CDs on special discs. The original type of CDR, known as a CD "burner" could not erase information once it had been written to the gold dye blank. Newer drives using $2 blanks can both record and erase information. These drives provide the ideal way to transfer large amounts of information between locations, because all of today's PCs are equipped with CD drives that can read these discs. Recorded CDs also provide extremely stable backups for long-term archiving of data that can still be quickly accessed, provided you can find the disc. The standard capacity of CD discs is 74 minutes stereo-quality music, or about 650 MB (about a sixth of the capacity of a small hard drive). All CD recorders can also play music CDs and read standard CD-ROMs, though their read speeds are appreciably lower than those of the much less expensive read-only drives.

DVD Drives

Digital video discs (DVDs) are another entertainment industry innovation, designed primarily for delivering a fourfold improvement in quality over VHS tapes for home movie distribution. DVDs hold from about 7 times as much information as CDs in their first incarnation to 28 times as much information (about 17 GB) in the double-layered, double-sided version. DVDs are expected to catch on in the PC industry faster than in home entertainment, due in part to the lack of an affordable recording function, but most software will continue to be delivered on CD for some time. Current DVD drives are a little slower than the state-of-the-art CDs, but the discs are the same size, and DVD drives can read manufactured CD discs, though not some discs recorded in CDRs. Unless you are a serious game player or really want to watch movies on your computer screen, a CDR is probably a more useful investment if you're prepared to go beyond a standard CD-ROM drive.

Tape Drives

Tape drives are the number one option for backing up business computer systems, though they have been edged out in home applications by cartridge-type disk drives from SyQuest and Iomega. The advantages of tape drives are high capacity and low media cost. Once you've paid for the tape drive, most tape cartridges are under $20 and can hold all of the data on your hard drive—a full backup, which in case of disaster can be used to restore your repaired or replaced PC to exactly the way you remember it. Since the tape cartridges are removable, you can keep one in your cookie jar or in a bank safety-deposit box if your data is that important. In a business, dozens of PCs can be backed up over a network at a single workstation by using multiple tapes. The main problem with backup tapes is access time. Unlike all of the other data storage media, which use some variation of a rotating circular disk to allow data anywhere on the disk to be located and read in a tiny fraction of a second, tapes need to be wound past the magnetic reading head. Restoring a single small file from a tape may take several minutes, depending on the length of the tape, the speed of the drive, and the location of the information. Making a new copy of an entire hard drive on tape can take hours.

Modems

Modems give your PC the ability to communicate with other computers over the phone lines or the cable TV system. For most people, this means connecting to the Internet and the World Wide Web or to work. Other uses for modems include using the PC as an answering machine, fax, or voice mail system, and for multiple-player games. One of the promises of PC technology that has not yet been widely realized is the ability of the PC, combined with the Internet and a few inexpensive extras, to make long-distance or international phone calls and videoconference calls using only local phone access. Modems, compared with most of the other parts in your PC, are extremely slow. Don't consider using anything slower than a 56-Kb/s (kilobits/second) modem. Newer cable modems allow you to access the Internet at much higher speeds by way of your cable TV supplier, although your cable franchise must support the option. Dedicated line modems, using an alphabet soup of technologies like ISDN (Integrated Services Digital Network) and ADSL (Asymmetric digital subscriber line), usually fall somewhere between 56-Kb/s modems and cable modems in performance while costing as much or more than cable modem service. Dedicated satellite dishes are another way to go, but you tie up your regular phone line for outgoing communications while using them. Some motherboards, like the one we used for the Pentium III system in this book, include an integrated 56-Kb/s modem as a standard feature.

Network Adapter

Everybody who works in an office environment is familiar with computer networks, or at least with computer networks being "down." A network adapter in your PC plays essentially the same role as a modem, but it operates much, much faster. The fastest modem, operating at 56,000 bits/second, is transferring up to 7000 bytes per second over the phone lines. The cheapest network adapter operating over a dedicated network of shielded phone lines in a building can transfer 10 Mb/s (10 million bits per second, or around 1.2 million bytes per second). So a slow network adapter transfers about as much information in one minute as does a fast modem in three hours! Because network adapters have gotten so inexpensive (as little as $10), and the new operating systems like Windows Millennium make it easy to build a small network, many two-computer families use a network in their homes to share a printer, play games, or back up information for safekeeping. These inexpensive networks, known as peer-to-peer, can provide peripheral sharing and even common Internet access to several computers for a total hardware investment under $100. One of the best reasons to include a network card in your home PC is to be prepared for connectivity to the Internet via high-speed devices, like an external cable modem, should the service become available in your area.

Sound Systems

Sound cards translate data stored on your PC or downloaded from the Internet into the analog sound waves we can hear, a process called *D/A (digital-to-analog) conversion*. Sound cards can also take the analog music or speech from a recording or microphone and rapidly sample it, creating a digital version of the sound for use on the PC, known as *A/D (analog-to-digital) conversion*. The primary items differentiating sound systems are the power and clarity of their amplifiers and speakers (i.e., will your PC sound as good as your stereo?). Similarly, cheap sound cards may not make as clear a recording as their brand-name brethren. However, the main marketing points for high-end sound cards are their "wave table sound" and "polyphony" components. *Wave table sound* allows a sound card to play a form of compressed music, commonly used with games or multimedia presentations, in which the "true" waveform of the sound desired is produced by the sound card from a wave table. *Polyphony* refers to how many independent sound streams the card can produce and mix at one instance.

The up-and-coming use of sound cards in PC systems is for "speech recognition"—that is; talking to your PC. Speech recognition allows for hands-off operation of your computer, with dictation directly to type being the leading application. The technology is rapidly improving, and finding acceptance with professionals in challenging environments such as medical offices and legal practices. Sound card capabilities are the most common candidate for integration into the motherboard, and two of the systems built in this book require no sound adapter.

Keyboard and Mouse

Two of the cheapest components attached to any computer system are the keyboard and the mouse, which taken together can cost less than $20. If there is any correlation between the cost of keyboards and the quality, it seems to be that the cheapest keyboards last the longest! Mice, on the other hand, are generally nicer as you move up the price ladder, but all mechanical mice require occasional cleaning. Cleaning a mouse is a five-minute job, normally undertaken when the screen pointer refuses to move where you want it to go. Keyboards are available in a variety of styles, from the standard 104/105-key rectangular keyboard to the split ergometric keyboard and the oversize "surfer" keyboards with dedicated Internet keys. The new PCs we build in this book use the small PS/2-style connector for both the mouse and the keyboard.

Figure 1.8

Microsoft Internet keyboard.

Figure 1.9

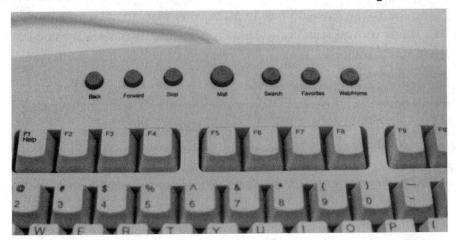

Web navigation keys.

The Video Monitor

The video monitor is often the most expensive component of a basic PC system, which isn't a bad thing because it's also the only component that comes close to retaining value over time. A monitor is very similar to an artist's canvas in that it presents no images or information on its own; instead, it needs to be painted by a remote hand or controller. The video adapter installed in your PC may only cost 10 percent as much as the monitor, yet it controls the resolution of the image and the number of colors displayed. Monitors, like televisions, are described by the diagonal measurement of the picture tube, in inches. All things being equal, when a 17-inch monitor displays the same image as a 14-inch monitor, the picture will appear to be almost 50 percent larger. However, the true viewable area of a monitor rarely reaches the actual picture tube measurements, depending on how much of the tube is covered by the plastic housing and whether or not the monitor controls let you adjust the picture out to the edges.

A basic understanding of the internal workings of a monitor is nice to have, but if you're buying inexpensive components, you don't need to worry about it. The data to be displayed on the screen is actually passed from the video adapter to the monitor in analog form, varying voltage levels to describe the intensity for the red, green, and blue electron guns to paint each point on the display. The monitor electronics steer the beams from these electron guns by use of *magnetic fields* (also called *lenses*), which deflect the beams down and across the screen at speeds determined by the vertical and horizontal refresh frequencies. The *vertical refresh rate* describes how many times the entire screen is redrawn in a second, and the horizontal frequency must be fast enough to steer the beam all the way across the screen enough times to paint every *pixel* (point on the screen) in a single vertical scan cycle. These refresh frequencies are included in the product information sheet for every monitor and high-performance video adapter, so it's a game of making sure the numbers match up.

Pixels provide a measure of image resolution (detail), with no dependence on the monitor used. A picture made up from a grid of 640 horizontal by 480 vertical points (640×480) is the lowest-quality image (plain VGA) used today, and this is sharper than a standard TV picture. Even the least-expensive monitors manufactured today can display much higher resolution (finer) images than this, but for many people, an inexpensive video adapter/monitor pairing flickers noticeably when pushed to higher-resolutions. The main factor controlling flicker is the vertical refresh frequency, and a monitor and adapter capable of 75 or 85 redraws per second at a given resolution (75 Hz or higher) will produce a really solid picture. The sharpness of the images painted, however, is dependent on the *dot pitch*, or *stripe pitch*, of the monitor phosphor. The *pitch* is a measure, in millimeters, of the distance between two phosphor dots or stripes of the same color on the inside surface of the monitor screen. Some manufacturers use an aperture or mask pitch measurement, which actually describes the size of the holes in part of the beam-focusing train, but an equivalent phosphor dot pitch measurement should be available. Actual dot pitch sizes still in use (forget about the bad old days) run from about 0.25 to 0.31 mm, all of which look good to me.

Monitors have slowly gotten cheaper, so that the 14-inch standard is now often sale priced below $100, and the entry-level 17-inch monitors start around $200. New thin-screen monitors, really large LCD displays similar to those used on notebook computers, are still far too expensive to be considered by most do-it-yourselfers.

Video Adapters

When it comes to choosing a video adapter, the Advanced Graphics Port (AGP) design is the only way to go. The main figure of merit for these video adapters is the amount of RAM they sport, which fixes the number of pixels and colors they can display, as detailed in the next chapter. AGP cards also have a basic speed rating of 1X, 2X, or 4X, which describes the maximum data transfer rate they can achieve in ideal circumstances. You can spend a lot of money on a video adapter intended for rapidly rendering high-resolution 3D graphics for animation. These adapters find their primary application in heavy imaging environments where the product is the picture, such as medical imaging, training simulators, graphics rendering,

Figure 1.10

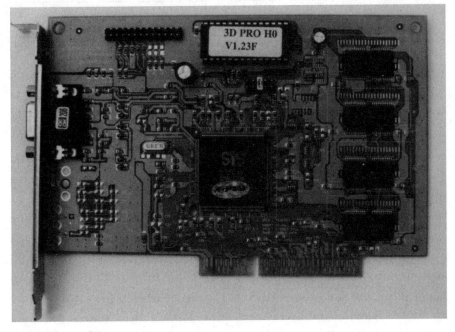

AGP video adapter.

and of course, games. For most home users, the standard $30 AGP adapter is more than adequate and, in many cases, actually less prone to compatibility problems than adapters costing five times as much. Their only drawback is that if you try connecting your monitor from 1992 or 1993 to your new AGP graphics card, it may not work, because the industry has gradually abandoned support for the standard modes of these older devices.

Many new motherboards come with "onboard video," an AGP video controller and monitor connection port integrated into the motherboard design, eliminating the need for a separate video adapter. Surprisingly, these motherboards often cost less than motherboards without video capabilities. We used such a motherboard to build the Pentium III/Celeron system in our book, but we should point out that there are three drawbacks to using them:

1. The capabilities of the integrated controller are often limited in comparison with even inexpensive video adapters.

2. The video adapter shares the main memory on the motherboard with the system. This means that if you have a system with 32 MB RAM, up to 8 MB may be stolen by the video controller, leaving only 24 MB for the operating system.

3. Manufacturers rarely include a slot for installing a regular AGP adapter, since they have already included video functions on the motherboard. Therefore, if the onboard video is insufficient or fails, it can only be replaced with an older PCI (Peripheral Component Interconnect) video adapter, or the motherboard will need replacing.

Printers and Scanners

Almost everyone will want to own a printer with their PC, and scanners are increasingly common purchases, as their prices have fallen well below that of printers. In short, a variety of color inkjet printers are available for between $150 and $300. Many have problems handling paper, and replacing the ink cartridges is a big hidden expense. When shopping for inkjets, go to a retail store that will let you print some test pages, and check the price of the cartridges, because you'll be buying more of them than you think. If you do a serious amount of printing (more than 10 pages a day), and you can live without color, buy a laser printer. Decent-quality black-and-white laser printers sell in the $400 to $600 price range. The more expensive models are intended for very high volume office usage, and the very inexpensive units share some of the paper-handling problems common to inkjets. Color laser printers have fallen in price to the low thousands range, but since they still cost more than the average PC, you'll want to research them carefully before buying. For scanners, unless you are a professional artist, the cheapest $50 model will probably make you happy, but check with the vendor for compatibility issues between printers and scanners that will share the same port. All scanners do a good job with color photographs—more than sufficient if your main use will be scanning images for the Internet. Just make sure you get a flatbed scanner if you plan on scanning documents for optical character recognition (OCR), a software application that changes the image of written words into text that you can import into your word processor.

Operating System (OS) Software

For most PC builders, the choice of operating system is similar to Henry Ford's famous Model T quote, "You can get it in any color as long as it's black." For those who want to be able to run all of the shrink-wrapped software sold in stores, you can buy any operating system, as long as it's Microsoft Windows. Most folks will be best off with Windows ME, but some will choose Windows 2000 or even the older Windows 98. There is a growing "anybody but Microsoft" movement, which has picked the freeware Linux operating system as its standard-bearer, and many people install multiple operating systems on their hard drives—the computer world version of having your cake and eating it, too. There are plenty of freeware software applications that run under Linux, including full business productivity suites, but don't expect to see it listed as an option on the side of the industry standard Microsoft Office box any time soon.

Table of Units

Unit shorthand	Unit written out	Actual value	Applies to	Nominal range
b	Bit	0 or 1, expressed as a small voltage	Bus width, memory module width	8, 16, 32, 64, 128
B	Byte	8 bits	Basic unit of capacity	Byte, kilobyte, megabyte, gigabyte
KB	Kilobyte	1000 bytes	File size	1 KB to megabytes
MB	Megabyte	1 million bytes	Capacity, CD, memory	1 MB to gigabytes
GB	Gigabyte	1 billion bytes	Capacity, hard drive, DVD	1 GB to terabytes
Kb/s	Kilobits/ second	1000 bits per second	Modem and I/O port speeds	14.4 to 112 Kb/s
Mb/s	Megabits/ second	1 million bits per second	Network and serial bus transfer speed	10 to 100 Mb/s
KB/s	Kilobytes/ second	1000 bytes per second	File download speed via modem	1 to 10 KB/s
MB/s	Megabytes/ second	1 million bytes per second	Hard drive and device bus (PCI, SCSI) transfer speed	3 to 160 MB/s
MHz	Megahertz	1 million cycles per second	CPU clock, bus clock	8 to 1000 MHz
ms	Milliseconds	1/1000 of a second	Drive seek time, keyboard repeat rate	5 to 300 ms
ns	Nanosecond	1 billionth of a second	Memory access speed	6 to 70 ns
d	Dot	A unique point	Computer screens	0.26 to 0.31 mm (as "dot pitch" of screen)
dpi	Dots/inch	Dots per inch printed or scanned	Printers, scanners	100 to 2400 dpi (typeset quality)

CHAPTER 2

Selecting and Purchasing Parts

In this chapter we will review the basic component choices you need to make before you begin purchasing parts. If you already have some experience with assembling PCs, the relationships between these parts will be clear to you. If not, we suggest that you take some time now to browse through the assembly photographs in Chapters 4 to 7 in order to see how PCs are actually put together. This will give you a little familiarity with the physical appearance of the parts, along with the sizing relationships and connections that will be made between the components, and enhance the usefulness of the material in this chapter.

There are three major sources for buying computer parts at good prices, and each has its advantages and disadvantages. The first source is mail order, based on parts lists and prices in magazine or Web advertisements. The main advantages of mail order are price, unlimited selection, and the security inherent in credit card transactions. The hidden time bomb of mail-order purchasing is shipping costs and turnaround time, both the initial cost to get the parts to you and any reshipping costs and delays due to mistakes or defective merchandise. One way to minimize shipping costs is to buy all of your parts from the same mail-order supplier. However, you must clearly state at the time of your order that you will not accept partial shipment or the delivery charges may start mounting up. Even worse, your order may show up lacking some critical component that may be another week in coming, effectively postponing the build. In extreme cases, partial shipments may be accepted and paid for, only for the supplier to call two weeks later and report that they no longer stock the missing part at all. The monitor you can buy anywhere, since it will ship in its own box regardless. Another problem with some mail-order outlets is that the prices you are quoted may mysteriously creep up a few bucks here and there. This will generally be attributed to "a problem in the system," and by reading your invoice and complaining, you can be sure to pay what you intended.

Another major source for parts is computer shows. Vendors at computer shows often have incredibly aggressive pricing, which makes you wonder if their merchandise fell off a truck. While shows don't have quite the variety of parts and vendors you will find in Ziff-Davis's *Computer Shopper* magazine, they do offer an interesting mix of the latest stuff and closeout items. One advantage of the shows is that you can see exactly what you are getting, and you can often get vendors to stick your part in a demo machine to prove that it's working properly. You'll also get plenty of free advice about what to buy and why, and you'll see a lot of things you'd like to have if money were no object. However, shows have a couple major drawbacks. For one thing, the cost for fly-by-night outfits to set up a booth at a computer show is appreciably less than the cost of an ad in a magazine. This means that anybody with $50 in his or her pocket can rent a table, put up a "Moe's Computer" sign, sell you stuff with a three-year warranty, and disappear off the face of the Earth on Monday. Another drawback is that the show atmosphere can lead to hastily made purchasing decisions, and many hyper-type salespeople who wouldn't last a week in a retail store are attracted to shows like sharks to a shipwreck.

The third source for reasonably priced computer parts is large retail computer stores, usually chains. The main advantage of retail stores is that if you get a defective part, you can usually return it for another one, hassle free. You can't expect to get a good deal on all of your parts in retail stores, but they often sell items such as hard drives and memory as loss leaders. The bigger chains can get pretty good deals from manufacturers on boxed items that move quickly (printers, monitors, and boxed hard drives), but beware of rebate schemes. Both personal experience and media reporting teach that many rebate offers go unfulfilled. If you do gamble on pricing backed by rebates, stick with big-name manufacturers, make photocopies of all of the documentation before sending it in, and mark down on a calendar the date by which you'll want to call up and start complaining. Never buy the store warranty!

A system including a case, power supply, motherboard, memory, and CPU is generally referred to as a *bare-bones system*. There is a big advantage to buying the bare bones of your system from a single source. First of all, the supplier accepts the responsibility that the components you buy will work together when assembled properly. This means you won't end up with a CPU that isn't supported by your particular motherboard model, that the memory you buy will operate at peak performance and not at some fall-back "basic compatibility," and that you won't end up with a mix of AT and ATX components. Another advantage is that if you have difficulty getting your assembled system to work, your vendor can't try to shift the blame to other suppliers. Unfortunately, this scenario of having something not work or fit properly out of the collection of parts you purchase to assemble your system is fairly common.

Paying for Performance

To do full justice to all of the new technologies and variations that are used in today's PCs, we would have to double or triple the number of pages in this book, and then you would have to sift through them! Our compromise is to supply enough information to enable you to make educated buying decisions for parts, and in a necessarily condensed form. You don't need to master all of the information and terms in this chapter to successfully build a PC; assembly requires very little knowledge about the parts themselves. A good vendor will help you choose the right combination of components for your performance needs and budget. No book can make you a purchasing expert until you get some hands-on experience, but hopefully the information in this chapter will help you ask the right questions before you lay out your hard-earned cash.

The hardest question you have to ask yourself when purchasing parts for your PC is, "How much performance do I need today?" There is no point in the computer game in trying to cover your possible future needs with what you buy today, particularly since you are building your own PC and can easily upgrade it a year from now when that $500 CPU you were considering costs $100. However, if you need the performance now, there's no choice other than to pay for it. Still, there are a couple points to keep in mind. Performance increases are rarely cumulative. In other words, if you buy five components (a CPU, a hard drive, a CD-ROM, a video adapter, and RAM), each of which guarantees you a 20 percent increase in performance, you won't end up with a PC that is 100 percent faster. You're more likely to end up with a PC that's 20 percent faster some of the time. Why not all of the time? Well, if you spend a lot of time surfing the Web, the pages aren't going to load any faster. The limiting factor there is your 56K modem. If you print a lot of color pictures on your inkjet, they won't print any faster. The real bottleneck there is the printer itself. What is cumulative about the five "high-performance" parts is the price. That hypothetical PC will cost twice as much. In fact, unless you are an avid game player, pushing motion 3D graphics to their limit, your PC spends most of its on time waiting for you to ask it to do something!

Case and Power Supply

The most important point to remember when buying components to build a new computer is to buy ATX standard components. All four of the PCs we build in this book will use an ATX standard case, power supply, and motherboard. The older AT standard cases are still widely available and might seem attractive at a few dollars cheaper, particularly as vendors try to liquidate their stock, but stay away from these. The ATX power supply comes with a large 20-wire connector that plugs into the motherboard, sev-

Figure 2.1

Fully assembled midtower.

eral 4-wire connectors in two sizes that supply power to your drives (floppy, hard drive, CD-ROM, or DVD), and an exterior connection for a power cord that is plugged into a standard electrical outlet. All of these connectors are keyed by their shape and the shape of the receptacles such that they can't go on the wrong way unless you really force them. The only exception is with some small drives (floppies and tape drives) that use the small-form drive connectors, and these should be labeled or shipped with instructions showing the proper orientation on the connector.

In this book, we will build two systems in ATX midtowers, one system in an ATX minitower, and one system in an ATX desktop. Before the advent of CD drives, you could always stand your desktop case on its side, creating an instant minitower. Now, with the presence of a CD drive in every system, this no longer works, because the tray that loads the CD disc into the drive works only in one orientation: upside up. The main advantages of a desktop case are that you can usually place your monitor on top of it, cutting down on desk space required, and it has a lower center of gravity if you're worried about the kids knocking it over. The main advantage of

Figure 2.2

Fully assembled desktop.

all tower systems (minitower, midtower, and tower) is that they are easier to assemble. To determine which type of case is right for you, it may be helpful to thumb through the assembly pictures for each system before you go out and buy the parts. Any of these systems could have been built in any of these cases, but you will see that there are always trade-offs, and one type of case may be better suited to a particular configuration than another.

The main figure of merit for power supplies is the power output, in watts (W). The typical ATX power supply sold in standard cases provides 250 W, divided between the motherboard and the drive power leads. With the exception of CPUs and CD recorders (CDRs), the power required by computer parts has actually been falling since the 250-W supply became stan-

Case type	Description	Drive bays	Power supply	Price
Minitower	Stands upright on desktop (12 to 18 inches high)	Two 5.25-inch, two or three 3.5-inch	250 W	$30 to $50
Midtower	Stands upright on desktop or floor (18 to 30 inches high)	Three or four 5.25-inch, three to seven 5.5-inch	250 to 300 W	$40 to $80
Desktop	Sits flat on desktop (6 to 8 inches high)	Two or three 5.25-inch, two or three 3.5-inch	250 W	$35 to $70
Tower	Stands upright on floor (24 to 36 inches high)	Four to six 5.25-inch, four to eight 3.25-inch	300 to 350 W	$75 to $150

dard. The second-most popular power supply is the 300 W, and these are commonly used in systems with dual CPUs, three or more hard drives, or some other power-hungry configuration. Avoid locking in to some of the mini-ATX designs and slim-line cases, which push the limit of how small a space you can cram a working PC into, and which offer extremely limited flexibility in choosing components and upgrading.

CPUs

Earlier in the chapter, we introduced motherboards before CPUs, because the CPU is mounted on the motherboard, and from an assembly approach, it's easier to understand constructing a house on a foundation than excavating a foundation under a house. However, when it comes to purchasing computer components, the choice of CPU determines which motherboard and memory you can buy, so choosing the CPU is really the first step. For better or for worse, the number of different CPUs to choose from is at an all-time high. The market is dominated by two manufacturers, Intel and AMD (Advanced Micro Devices), and each of these produces two different families of CPUs that are in widespread use. The flagship processor of Intel is the Pentium III, and the new contender to the throne is the AMD Athlon. The companies also produce CPUs for the low-cost PC market, the Intel Celeron and the AMD Duron and K6-2, which are more than adequate for the average user. After you mount the CPU and install the memory on the motherboard, about a five-minute job, the parts and procedures for assembling any of these types of PCs are essentially identical. We chose to fully illustrate the assembly of four complete systems in different cases to clearly illustrate the largest possible number of options.

Each type of CPU comes in a different "package" that describes how the CPU is connected to the motherboard. Only two of these CPUs, the

Pentium III and the Celeron, are currently available in two different packages. CPU prices are structured to take advantage of business buyers for whom a few hundred dollars in cost difference is a small factor in the overall purchasing decision. Never buy the fastest-speed CPU within a family of processors, or you'll be paying several hundred dollars extra for a speed differential that is impossible to detect in most applications. If you have the extra money to spend, consider using it on options with far more impact, like a larger monitor, better printer, more memory, and so on. When it comes to choosing between CPUs of the same price and speed rating (MHz), it's hard to go wrong by closing your eyes and pointing. Modern PCs can be loosely divided into families by their CPU packages and their corresponding motherboard receptacles, which in order of historical introduction are Socket 7, Slot 1 and Slot 2, Socket 370, and Slot A.

CPUs should not be chosen for their internal architectural design features. These are entirely transparent to the user. Terms like superscalar and superpipelined, multiple-branch prediction, and out-of-order processing describe advances that are used in all of the current CPU designs; they do not provide a basis for comparison. All of the CPUs in current production that are discussed in this book are fully x86 binary code–compatible (they will work with software written for any PC since the IBM-AT) and support industry-standard MMX (Multi-Media eXtension) instructions. This means they will be capable of running any shrink-wrapped software package you might buy. There are really only three factors to take into consideration when choosing a new CPU: the price, the speed (in MHz), and bus support. For example, if you have already decided that you want to build a system using the new 133-MHz memory bus, you've already limited your choice to CPUs with a 133-MHz frontside bus (FSB) rating. When comparing CPU pricing, don't forget to take the cost of the motherboard into account. For example, the motherboard cost for the Pentium III system (with a Celeron option) that we build in Chapter 4 was $80, and this included onboard AGP video, sound, 10/100BaseT network, and even a V.90 modem. The motherboard for the Athlon system we build in Chapter 5 cost $150, and only includes onboard sound.

Socket 7

There are more Socket 7 CPUs still in use than any other kind, and although this technology has been officially updated to a new standard known as "Super 7," we are following the standard industry practice in continuing to use the "Socket 7" nametag. There are currently two high-performance, cost-effective CPUs available for Socket 7, the AMD K6-2 and the AMD K6-3. AMD has continued improving the K6-2, such that at press time, it is available in higher-speed versions than the K6-3. Socket 7 motherboards are manufactured with a fixed amount of L2 cache memory (Level 2 or secondary) that is tightly coupled with the CPU, usually 1 or 2 MB. Socket 7

Figure 2.3

AMD K6 next to Socket 7.

motherboards are usually the least expensive option for the home computer builder, and due to their long market presence, are available in a tremendous variety. We completely assemble a Socket 7 PC with a K6 series CPU
in Chapter 7.

Slot 1 and Slot 2

Intel Pentium III, Pentium II, and Celeron processors are designed for Slot
1 motherboards. The Pentium III and Celeron are also available in a Socket
370 package. The Pentium III Xeon and Pentium II Xeon are Slot 2 CPUs
that are targeted for the high-end workstation and server market. Slot 1 and

Figure 2.4

Intel Pentium II in Slot 1.

Slot 2 CPUs are not interchangeable, and for the time being, Slot 2 systems are too pricey for all but the most demanding commercial applications. The procedures for building Slot 1-based systems with the different CPU choices are nearly identical. The Pentium III and Pentium II systems in this book both utilize Slot 1 connectors.

Socket 370

The two CPUs currently available in the Socket 370 package are the Pentium III and the Celeron. Socket 370 and Socket 7 CPUs and sockets look similar, but they are not interchangeable. Socket 370 CPUs are less expensive than their Slot 1 twins, due to the simpler packaging and lack of discrete cache added to the CPU cartridge. Socket 370 CPUs have an increased amount of cache on the chip die, 128 KB or more, which allows designers to forgo adding external cache to their motherboards. The Celeron option built in Chapter 4 demonstrates Socket 370.

Slot A

The AMD Athlon is the latest entry into the desktop CPU market, and at its introduction, it actually anticipated the availability of some components. For example, the Athlon Slot A design is capable of operating the front-side memory bus memory at speeds double that of the Pentium III, but at press time, the memory required to achieve these gains was not widely available. The Athlon package is physically similar to Slot 1 CPUs, but they are mutually incompatible with each other's slot mounts. Chapter 5 details an Athlon Slot A build.

CPU	Package Type	Speed Rating	FSB speed (Front Side Bus)	Basic Price/Top performance price
Intel Pentium III Xeon	Slot 2	550 MHz +	100 MHz	$1000/$2000
Intel Pentium III	Slot 1/Socket 370	450 MHz +	133 or 100 MHz	$200/$700
AMD Athlon	Slot A/Socket A	500 MHz +	200 MHz	$180/$800
Intel Pentium II	Slot 1	350 MHz +	100 MHz	$100/$150
AMD Duron	Slot A/Socket A	600 MHz +	200 MHz	$120/$200
AMD K6-3	Socket 7	400 MHz +	100 MHz	$75/$150
Intel Celeron	Slot 1/Socket 370	333 MHz +	66 MHz	$45/$100
AMD K6-2	Socket 7	300 MHz +	100 or 66 MHz	$35/$110

Cache Memory

Once data is brought to the CPU and stored in the internal cache, it can be crunched away at the basic clock speed of the chip, somewhere between 400 and 1000 MHz for most current-generation computers. However, the amount of internal cache on the CPU, between 32 and 64 KB (kilobytes) of combined data and instruction cache, is many orders of magnitude below the size of the average program (megabytes) or average hard drive (gigabytes). The internal cache is usually supplemented by secondary or L2 (level 2) cache, normally 1 or 2 MB. Often called *external cache*, the secondary cache system employs static RAM (SRAM), which is four or five times faster than DRAM and doesn't require refreshing and all of the overhead that refreshing incurs. It's also many times more expensive than DRAM, which explains its limited use in PCs. Socket 370 CPUs, as previously mentioned, are designed with increased on-chip cache, and no support for L2 cache. The Pentium Xeon processors can transfer data from their tightly coupled external cache at the same clock speed as the CPU core.

Motherboards

There are currently four families of ATX motherboards being manufactured to support the four families of CPUs discussed earlier. These motherboards are compatible only with the CPU style they are designed for: You cannot install a Pentium II on a Socket 7 motherboard or an AMD K6-3 on a Slot 1 motherboard. In addition to the CPU, motherboards support various types and amounts of memory (RAM), though the tremendous flexibility built into most new motherboards and the plummeting cost of the latest memory modules has made this a simpler issue for the new computer builder than it was a few years ago. There are two new memory technologies that require specific motherboard support, the ultra high speed RAMBUS modules and the double data rate SDRAM (synchronous DRAM). However, at press time, RAMBUS modules cost about eight times as much as SDRAM modules and double data rate SDRAM modules were not yet available. Older motherboards may not support the newer PC-133 SDRAM either, and this is another factor to take into account when price shopping CPUs and motherboards.

All of the new ATX motherboards come with a number of useful controllers built onto the board, which years ago had to be purchased and installed separately. For example, the parallel port for hooking up your printer, scanner, or inexpensive external drive is included on the motherboard, along with a port for hooking up your PS/2-style keyboard and mouse, a joystick, and two serial ports for hooking up slower general-purpose devices such as modems, digital cameras, and plotters. ATX designs include two universal serial bus (USB) ports, a relatively new general-purpose connection scheme for medium-speed devices that has yet to achieve great popularity with consumers. Three of the four motherboards used for builds in this book include an onboard sound controller, which replaces an add-in sound card adapter. You can purchase motherboards that include many other built-in features, including a video adapter, network adapter, modem, and so on. Integrated functionality is usually cheaper than purchasing individual adapters, and sometimes these options are essentially free. There are some drawbacks to integrated adapters, primarily with installing the latest operating system releases or when upgrading video capabilities. Most of the motherboard connection ports are attached to the back edge of the motherboard and exposed through a standard ATX opening, so the motherboard manufacturer must supply a custom metal shield that has openings for the exact number and arrangement of ports.

The memory bus gives the CPU access to the main memory, somewhere between 64 and 256 MB on the typical new system. The speed of the memory bus is one of the main factors differentiating new motherboards. Until fairly recently, the maximum speed of the memory bus was 66 MHz (megahertz = million cycles/sec). A 100-MHz memory bus designed to work with SDRAM became available with newer Slot 1 and Slot 2 and Socket 7 (or Super 7) motherboards, followed by a 133-MHz bus in the past year. In order for you to get the benefit of the 100-MHz or 133-MHz memory bus, you must purchase both a CPU and memory that are designed to take advantage of it. Both CPUs and RAM are generally backward-compatible, meaning they can run at slower speeds than they are optimally designed for; however, pushing them beyond their stated specification, a process known as "overclocking," is strictly a "proceed at your own risk" undertaking.

There are three different types of adapter card connectors on most new ATX motherboards, known as *bus slots*: ISA, PCI, and AGP. Since the number of bus slots that can be placed on a motherboard is limited by real estate considerations, motherboard manufacturers offer different mixes of these. If you are planning to reuse some adapters from an older PC, such as a scanner interface or video-capture card, you should pay close attention to the number of ISA slots, since some designs abandon them completely. The highly integrated motherboard used for the Pentium III build in Chapter 4 offers only one shared PCI/ISA slot, meaning a maximum of one adapter of any kind can ever be added to the system.

The 16-bit Industry Standard Architecture (ISA) bus has been around since the mid-1980s, so you might think that it would be obsolete. However, devices such as modems and sound cards simply don't need a higher-performance bus interface. Even the fastest modems use only half of the data connections available in the ISA slot. The trend is to produce these adapters as PCI simply because there are more PCI slots available on new motherboards than ISA slots. The main difference between today's ISA adapters and those used 10 years ago is the advent of Plug and Play. Modems and sound cards that are 100 percent Plug and Play have no jumpers or switches to set. They are configured by software once the operating system is installed. This isn't always such a good thing, since the adapters sometimes demand the same resources or refuse to accept settings you would like them to use. These problems are less common when building new PCs than when doing upgrades later on.

The Peripheral Component Interconnect (PCI) bus is used today for almost all of the high-performance adapters you purchase for your computer. Controllers that are integrated on your motherboard, for example, the hard drive controllers, use the PCI bus directly, with no add-in adapters required. PCI adapters tend to be easier to install than ISA adapters, which often require a good amount of force for insertion. You should always buy PCI adapters rather than ISA adapters wherever possible. The PCI bus is easier to manage, the Plug and Play implementation is much better, and the basic performance is eight times that of the ISA bus.

The Advanced or Accelerated Graphics Port (AGP), as its name implies, is really a port rather than a bus, but the motherboard connector appears very similar to a PCI slot. There can be only one AGP slot on the motherboard, and this is placed as close to the CPU and memory as possible. The AGP slot is actually a port on the memory bus, shared with the CPU. This allows an AGP video adapter to transfer or operate on images stored in main memory without encountering the speed bottleneck of the 33-MHz PCI bus. Another advantage of using the AGP port for your video adapter is reduced traffic on the PCI bus, which functions independently.

Motherboard Chipsets

Many books and magazines differentiate motherboards by the chipset they use. A *chipset* is a couple of branded, highly interdependent integrated circuits (ICs) that include all of the basic functionality that defines a PC, rather than a proprietary computer that happens to be built with a given CPU. Chipset manufacturers often provide complete motherboard plans to the motherboard manufacturers who buy them, such that motherboard manufacturers are often just names on the box. Their whole production process may be contracted out; no in-house engineering or support need exist. In the end, the chipset guarantees nothing, other than that the motherboard makers had the opportunity to implement the features supported by the chipset. How well they support all of the chipset features depends on the design and cost of the motherboard. Motherboards are equipped

Motherboard	CPU Type/ Speed	Bus Speed/ Chipset	Maximum Memory/ Configuration	Bus Slots	Special Features	Price
Asus XG	Slot 2 (Xeon)/ 550 MHz	100 MHz/ Intel 440 GX	2048 MB/ 4 DIMMs	1 ISA. 5 PCI, 1 AGP	Adaptec Ultra Wide SCSI, Intel 100BaseT	$550
FIC SD	Slot A (Athlon)/ 500 to 800 MHz	133 or 100 MHz/AMD 751	768 MB/ 3 DIMMs	1 ISA. 5 PCI, 1 AGP	UDMA/66	$140
Intel CC820	Slot 1/500 to 750 MHz	133 or 100 MHz/Intel 820	512 MB/ 2 DIMMs	5 PCI, 1 AGP	UDMA/66	$150
Tyan Trinity 400	Socket 370/ 433 to 750 MHz	133, 100, or 66 MHz/VIA Apollo Pro 133A	768 MB/ 3 DIMMs	1 ISA, 6 PCI, 1 AGP	UDMA/66	$100
Shuttle HOT 591	Super 7/233 to 500 MHz	100 or 66 MHz/VIA Apollo MVP3	256 MB/ 2 DIMMs	3 ISA, 3 PCI, 1 AGP		$75
LMR PC-100	Slot 1 and Socket 370/ 233 to 550 MHz	100 or 66 MHz/SiS	384 MB/ 3 DIMMs	1 ISA, 1 PCI (shared)	AGP video, sound 56-KBs V.90 modem, 10BaseT	$80

with a small amount of permanently stored software called the *basic input/output system* (BIOS). This software tells the hardware how to talk to the various components in the system and runs the power management and other low-level hardware tasks. The BIOS on all new motherboards is upgradeable with software from the manufacturer.

The only way to shop for motherboards is to compare, item for item, their listed features: CPU types supported, CPU speeds supported, memory bus speed supported, AGP bus speed supported, number of ISA slots, number of PCI slots, number and type of memory sockets and total memory supported, power management features, onboard controllers and ports, and, of course, the ATX form factor. The earliest chipsets available to motherboard manufacturers for supporting new processor/memory combinations are usually supplied by the CPU manufacturer to encourage adoption of the CPU. Intel is currently producing chipsets that support RAMBUS technology, while AMD is working on chipsets to support double data rate SDRAM. Aftermarket chipsets appear soon afterwards, and these compete with the original chipsets on price and feature support.

There are hundreds of ATX motherboards currently in production. The following table gives a few examples. Newer motherboards should support Ultra DMA/66 with the onboard IDE controller.

Memory Types

Dynamic random access memory (DRAM) has been the mainstay of PC memory since it first appeared in the early 1980s. The main attractions of DRAM are lower unit cost and lower power consumption. It's slower and more complicated to use than static random access memory (SRAM), which was actually invented first. DRAM takes advantage of a peculiarity of transistor physics to temporarily store a capacitive charge (your data bit) on one of the transistor leads. Since this charge dissipates in a matter of milliseconds, the data bit must be reread and recharged every couple hundredths of a second. This refreshing process is carried on by a dedicated controller, but the overhead involved carries a performance penalty. Today's DRAM is more than five times faster than that used in the original PC, and the 1-bit-wide 64-KB dual inline package (DIP) chip has given way to the 64-bit-wide 64-MB dual inline memory module (DIMM). SRAM is more expensive in terms of both price and real estate, so it is generally used in small amounts for cache.

Fast Page Memory (FPM) was the first big performance enhancement to DRAM, which previously treated each memory bank transaction like reinventing the wheel. FPM makes it faster to access data in the same memory "page," though the term *row* offers a better representation of what actually goes on. When a new data bit is to come from the same matrix row as the previous bit, the memory controller need only increment the column location, and the same row address will be used, saving a transaction.

Extended Data Out (EDO) DRAM shortens the recovery time between sequential RAM reads, offering up to a 20 percent performance boost in overall memory throughput. EDO is backward-compatible, meaning in most cases it will function in systems that support only FPM RAM, but there will be no performance gain unless the motherboard and BIOS specifically support EDO access. Burst EDO (BEDO) is the next level of performance in which a series, or burst, of bytes from memory are transferred to the CPU with a single request. If the CPU actually requires the next sequential memory address in the following fetch, an operation has been saved.

Synchronous DRAM (SDRAM) can really boost memory bandwidth through synchronizing itself with the system clock. This eliminates the vast majority of timing delays, which can result in wait states being taken by the CPU. The motherboard and BIOS must be designed for SDRAM for it to be installed. You may have to set the DIMM slot voltage on the motherboard with a jumper to either 5 or 3.3 V. Don't get confused between SDRAM and SRAM, despite the similarity in names. SDRAM is a member of the inexpensive, slower, dynamic RAM family, while SRAM refers to the more expensive static RAM technology.

Double Data Rate (DDR) is the next step for SDRAM, a technology that can effectively double the throughput of previous SDRAMs by transferring data on both rising and falling clock pulses. The new Athlon chipsets being designed by AMD will support DDR to maximize the performance of the 200-MHz FSB capability of the Athlon.

RAMBUS technology represents a complete departure from the step-by-step evolution of RAM we have presented to this point. Intel has already implemented RAMBUS technology in their newest chipset, and RAMBUS Inline Memory Modules (RIMMs) are commercially available as both brand-name and generic parts. However, with a price tag about eight times that of SDRAM, RIMMs are currently being used exclusively in commercial servers and high-end workstations.

Parity and ECC RAM

Two different methods are in common use for catching errors in RAM. The same techniques are also used to monitor data integrity on all sorts of bus transfers within your computer or serial transfers over your modem. *Parity* is a relatively straightforward system in which an extra parity bit is added to each byte, and this bit is set to 0 or 1, depending on whether the number of set bits in the data byte is even or odd. However, in the case of a failed parity check, the memory controller has no way of determining which bit was wrong, so it can ask only that the data be retransmitted or halt the system with a parity error. Also, if two bits in the same byte with different values flip, the parity check will report no error, since the byte-comparison value remains even or odd. Many PCs that use parity memory include an option in CMOS to turn off parity checking and will work with SIMMs (Single Inline Memory Modules) that lack the extra parity bit.

Error-correction code (ECC) memory, as the name implies, is capable of actually correcting single-bit errors on the fly and catching multiple-bit errors. Because this requires more extra bits per byte and extra data lines back to the memory controller, ECC RAM is more expensive to manufacture and implement. However, with memory prices falling so rapidly, ECC RAM has become much more affordable and is no longer used exclusively in servers or engineering workstations. A new development called ECC onboard DIMM (EOD) simplifies the motherboard circuitry, but it is overkill for the average home PC.

The systems in this book are all built with commercially available SDRAM. The original SDRAM modules for 66-MHz operation are populated with chips rated at 12 or 10 ns (nanoseconds); PC-100 modules must be populated with chips rated 8 ns, and PC-133 modules with chips rated

6 ns. If you have a large quantity of EDO RAM from an old system you are upgrading, or you can't resist some closeout sale of the stuff, many motherboards still support EDO. SDRAM is generally rated as being between 20 and 50 percent faster than EDO, depending on the bus speed and application. The 6 to 12 ns rating of SDRAM is not a direct comparison with the 60 or 70 ns rating of EDO.

Figure 2.5

DIMM and SIMM.

All motherboards, independent of the number of DIMM slots available, place limitations on the total amount of RAM that can be installed and the mix and positioning of the modules that are permissible. The notches in the contact edge of the DIMM not only prevent the modules from being installed backwards, they also describe the module voltage (3.3 or 5 V) and whether the memory is buffered or unbuffered. However, module speed and other factors prevent this from being a surefire way of determining DIMM compatibility, so either buy the memory and the motherboard from the same outfit, or buy the motherboard first so you can check the documentation. The price of memory is less than $1 per megabyte, depending on module capacity and speed. A 64-MB PC-100 or PC-133 module currently goes for about $60, with a premium for ECC. Memory prices are subject to violent price swings, so check the latest pricing before making any decisions.

Drive Basics

Hard drives are still faster in every way than optical drives, including CD-ROM and DVD. The two main figures of merit for any drive with spinning media are its *random access time* (in milliseconds (MS), or thousandths of a second), which describes how long it takes the drive to get the read head positioned over the location of your data, and the *maximum transfer rate*, which is a measure of how fast (in megabytes/second) the drive can make data available to the controller. Most drives come with a small onboard cache that works in two ways. If the drive is operating slower than the interface speed, the cache can be quickly filled and the CPU can go on to do other things while the hard drive or CDR writes the information to disk. A minimum of 1 MB of cache is particularly important in the case of CDRs, because they cannot be interrupted in the course of a write session or the disc is ruined. In the case of a superfast hard drive running on a slow interface or supplying previously requested information while the CPU is busy doing something else, the cache acts as a temporary storage place for the data. Controllers and drives using advanced direct memory access (DMA) modes avoid the latter problem, because the CPU is out of the transfer loop.

Hard drives are generally categorized by their spindle speed (rotational rate) and their interface. The lowest-performance hard drives in current production have a spindle speed of 5400; the fastest nearly double this at 10,000. The maximum transfer rates of the newest EIDE and SCSI interfaces outstrip the drive's maximum physical transfer rate, and you're often paying for prestige rather than performance. The average access time of new hard drives is well under 10 ms. (The emphasis placed on this figure of merit has lessened as improvements have slowed.) CD-ROMs, on the other hand, are now reaching average access times in the 70-ms area, an improvement of about five times over as many years. The transfer rates on CDs, expressed as a multiple of the original 150-KB/s transfer rate of a music CD drive, have now gone past 40X, or 6.0 MB/s.

Drive Interfaces and Performance: IDE and SCSI

Intelligent or Independent Drive Electronics (IDE) won the battle for the PC hard drive back in 1992, rendering all other standards except for Small Computer System Interface (SCSI) obsolete. SCSI was able to hang around due in part to its greater flexibility in high-end computers (up to seven drives or devices could be attached to a controller, and greater data rates were possible) and partly because the Apple Macintosh used SCSI devices exclusively, which created a market outlet for manufacturers. Even today, if you're building a PC for anything other than a network server or a high-end workstation, you'll want to use the Enhanced or Extended IDE (EIDE) support built into the motherboard. In the case of newest EIDE and SCSI interfaces, the high transfer rates are achieved only when the data is being transferred from the on-drive cache. However, with EIDE, both hard drives and CD-ROMs are cheaper, and the controller interface is free, built right into the motherboard. There are other ways of connecting drives to a system. An enhanced printer port (EPP), also known as an extended capability port (ECP), is often used for connecting removable media drives or inexpensive scanners; large computers often employ serial fiber-optic buses.

IDE and ATA

The original IDE interface was defined by the ATA (AT Attachment, as in PC-AT) standard, adopted by the American National Standards Institute (ANSI), and amounted to little more than some buffering between the system I/O bus and the IDE drive, which has an onboard controller. The two-drive interface did allow for a secondary channel, which would take another interrupt and additional address space. So IDE and ATA refer to the same thing, and numbered versions of ATA refer to subsequent enhancements of the standard. The ATA Packet Interface (ATAPI) is a major upgrade that extends the ability of the interface to work with CDs, DVDs, and tape drives. The EIDE, which I use somewhat generically, if incorrectly, is actually a Western Digital trademark for their ATA implementation. Fast-ATA is a term coined by Seagate. Both support PIO mode 3 or better and DMA mode 1 or better (see following table). Ultra DMA/66 is one of the newest DMA tricks already incorporated into new ATX motherboards. UDMA/66 or Ultra ATA is the first IDE implementation that requires a change in the old 40-conductor IDE ribbon cable. The UDMA/66 cable retains the 40-pin cable header (connector), but the ribbon cable itself uses 80 conductors, with the addition of a ground between every signal wire for noise immunity.

Figure 2.6

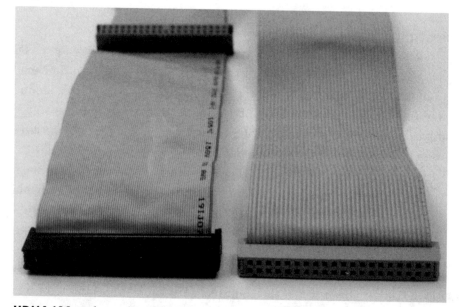

UDMA/66 and regular IDE ribbon cables.

The EIDE interface supports up to four drives: a master and slave on each of two channels. Both the interface and the EIDE drives are built with varying capabilities, though backward compatibility can usually be taken for granted. The basic, no-frills, or special BIOS support speed of the IDE or ATA interface is around 3.3 MB/s (megabytes/second). This is good enough to keep up with a 22X CD-ROM or most hard drives with the old 3600-rpm spindle speed (3600 disc revolutions per minute). The intermediate programmed or processor I/O (PIO) modes and direct memory access (DMA) modes used by EIDE and Fast-ATA are big performance boosters. The highest-performance modes are somewhat vaporware-like, because the drives that can produce these transfer rates don't exist. There are five possible PIO modes and four DMA modes, as shown in the following table.

Transfer Type	Mode	Transfer Rate
PIO	Mode 0	3.3 MB/s
PIO	Mode 1	5.2 MB/s
PIO	Mode 2	8.3 MB/s
PIO	Mode 3	11.1 MB/s
PIO	Mode 4	16.6 MB/s
DMA	Mode 1	13.3 MB/s
DMA	Mode 2	16.6 MB/s
DMA	Ultra/33	33 MB/s
DMA	Ultra/66	66 MB/s

SCSI Interface and Drives

The Small Computer Systems Interface (SCSI) is actually the oldest (and still champion) standard in use for connecting drives and high-performance peripherals to PCs. With the exception of the cheapest SCSI throwaway adapters sometimes shipped with proprietary CD drives or scanners, all SCSI adapters support up to 7 devices (14 for SCSI-2), in any combination, including those internal and external to the system box. SCSI devices all remain backward-compatible. You should be able to attach the newest devices to your oldest controller, though you'll lose any performance benefits that would have been due to the higher SCSI support of the device and a special cable may be required. The SCSI bus is inherently more reliable than the IDE interface, due in part to the large number of grounds used in SCSI cables to provide protection against electrical noise. SCSI devices that are commonly available in both internal and external versions include hard drives, tape backups, CD-ROMs, CDRs, and optical drives. The most common external-only SCSI peripheral is the scanner, though cheaper scanners are increasingly relying on the enhanced printer port.

Level	Known As	Number of Devices	Maximum Transfer Speed	Bus Width
SCSI-1	SCSI	7 (8 w/controller)	5 MB/s	8 bits
SCSI-2	Fast SCSI	7	10 MB/s	8 bits
	Fast Wide SCSI	15 (16 w/controller)	20 MB/s	16 bits
SCSI-3	Ultra SCSI	7	20 MB/s	8 bits
	Ultra Wide SCSI	15	40 MB/s	16 bits
	Ultra-2 SCSI	7	40 MB/s	8 bits
	Ultra-2 Wide SCSI	15	80 MB/s	16 bits
	Ultra-3 SCSI	7	80 MB/s	8 bits
	Ultra-3 Wide SCSI	15	160 MB/s	16 bits

SCSI devices are usually among the simplest to install, with termination being the sole wild card. SCSI devices require termination at both ends of the bus to absorb leftover power, which prevents reflections of the radio frequency signals within the transmission line. If the SCSI adapter is found in the middle of the bus, when both internal and external devices are installed, it must have its terminators removed or software disabled. Internal SCSI devices come with either resistor packs to be removed for an unterminated device (old style) or a single jumper on newer devices. External SCSI devices may provide a switch for termination, but more commonly they require installation of a snap-on terminator on the outgoing side of a daisy-chained port. Some SCSI devices are available in the "differential bus" bus flavor, which further increases noise immunity and allows longer distances for external devices, but these cannot be mixed with standard SCSI devices, and they follow their own termination rules.

DVD Drives and Technology

Much like CD-ROM before it, DVD has come to the computer industry by way of the entertainment industry. CDs were originally designed for the music industry, and over the course of a decade they replaced the old LPs. CDs didn't begin a new life as data storage devices for computers until long after they were an established winner in home audio. DVDs are designed (primarily) as a higher-quality, harder-to-pirate replacement for the VHS tapes and LaserDiscs currently used to distribute movies. Unlike CDs, DVDs are expected to have their greatest initial success as data storage devices for PCs, replacing VCRs only gradually. Part of the reason is cost; another factor is that there is currently no reasonable way for homeowners

Drive Type	Capacity Range	Interface	Recommended Brand Names	Notes	Price Range
Hard drive	6 to 40 GB	IDE (UDMA/66)	Western Digital, Seagate, Maxtor, Quantum, IBM	5400 or 7200	$85 to $500—price rises with capacity, spindle speed
Hard drive	6 to 60 GB	SCSI Ultra Wide, Ultra SCSI, Ultra SCSI 2	Seagate, Western Digital, Quantum	7200 or 10,000 RPM	$200 to $1000—price rises with capacity and interface, speed
CD Drive	680 MB	IDE	Mitsumi, ACER, Toshiba	44X or higher	$30 to $75 based on speed
CD drive	680 MB	SCSI	Plextor, NEC, Toshiba	32X or higher	$75 to $100 based on speed
CD Recorder	680 MB (74 minutes)	IDE, SCSI, USB	Mitsumi, Toshiba, Plextor, Ricoh, HP, Yamaha	4 to 8X write, 8 to 22X read	$150 to $500 based on speed, cache. Blank discs $2.
DVD drive	18 GB (must eject to turn over double-sided discs)	IDE or SCSI	Toshiba, Sony, Hitachi, Pioneer	40X reading CD, 6X reading DVD	$75 to $150, higher price for kit with movie decoder
Travan tape drive	2 to 10 GB (use 4-mm DAT for higher capacity)	IDE, SCSI, printer port	Seagate, HP	Reliable but slow	$15 to $450 depending on capacity; $30 per tape
Zip drive	100 MB	ISE, SCSI, printer port	Iomega	Quick backup	$75 to $100, depending on interface; $10 per cartridge
Floppy drive	1.44 MB; 120-MB Super Floppy (LS 120) available	Floppy	Mitsumi, Teac, Sony, Chinon, Panasonic	Regular floppy cheap; Super Floppy not widely used	$15; Super Floppy for $75

to record television shows on DVD. The giants of the entertainment industry continue to battle over the DVD standard, worries over piracy abound, and the whole thing could still go the way of Betamax versus VHS.

The technology of DVDs is very similar to that of CDs, and for the time being, CDs are actually faster than DVDs. A dual-speed DVD has a native data transfer rate of approximately an 18X CD, and the single-speed DVD data rate is equivalent to a 9X CD. DVD players for computers are available in EIDE (ATAPI) and SCSI flavors, starting at around $75. DVD capacity is about 4.7 GB per layer per side, with one or two layers per side, for a maximum of around 18 GB. Two-sided discs must be ejected and turned over manually. All DVD players can read manufactured CD-ROMs, but some may have problems with CDR discs. There are two types of DVD recorders available for PCs: DVD-RAM and DVDR. Both are good for recording data, not movies, and they fall short of 4 GB per side. Various copy-protection schemes may make future DVD movie discs unvieweable in some current drives. A DVD audio standard is not yet finalized, and will probably be very slow to catch on, given the good quality and current installed base of CD stereos.

Video Adapter and Monitor

The main difficulty that most people encounter in their video subsystem is in the wrong resolution/color driver being selected for a given software application. Almost all video cards installed in systems today feature 8 MB of video memory, which is more than enough to display 24-bit true color (16.7 million colors) at the 800×600 resolution, the highest you'll normally want to run on a 14- or 15-inch screen. However, the default choice for most video drivers on installation is still 256 colors—go figure. In Windows 95/98, this is easily changed in Control Panel Monitor, or by clicking on the little monitor in the tray at the bottom right corner of the screen. Even more-brilliant true color uses 32 bits for more than 4 billion colors.

Resolution	Number of Pixels	Video RAM Required for 24-bit True Color	Video Monitor Size Recommended
640×480	307,200	1 MB	14 to 17 inch
800×600	480,000	2 MB	15 to 17 inch
1024×768	786,432	4 MB	17 to 21 inch
1152×870	1,002,240	4 MB	17 to 21 inch
1600×1200	1,920,000	8MB	19 inch or larger

Monitor size	Price*		Video Adapter	Price*
14 inch	$100 to $200		4 MB PCI	$25 to $50
15 inch	$125 to $250		4 MB AGP	$30 to $75
17 inch	$200 to $400		8 MB PCI	$40 to $90
19 inch	$350 to $1000		8 MB AGP	$30 to $100
21 inch	$700 to $2000		16 MB AGP	$75 to $200
23 inch +	$1000 +		32 MB AGP	$100 to $300

*Pricing for monitors increases with quality, brand, scan rates, and viewable area. Pricing for adapters increases with brand and 3D acceleration

Figure 2.7

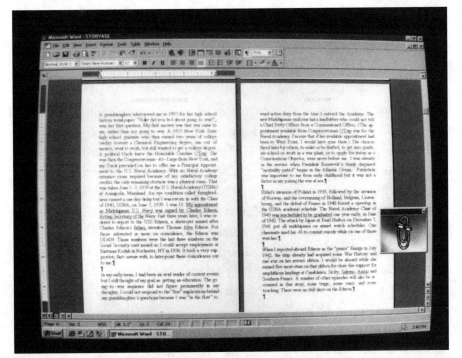

17-inch monitor with two-page display.

56-Kb/s Modems

There is no reason today to put anything other than a 56-Kb/s modem in a new PC. This doesn't guarantee that you'll get anywhere near 56 Kb/s when you connect, but given the prices and the probability that your Internet service provider (ISP) will upgrade in the near future, the older

Figure 2.8

56-Kb/s modem.

V.34 (33-Kb/s) modem is a waste of money. There are currently three standards for 56-Kb/s modems, which are implemented in software (firmware)
both on your modem and at the ISP. The original x2 standard introduced
by U.S. Robotics (acquired by 3COM) and the k56flex standard from
Rockwell and Lucent are not compatible with each other, nor with the V.90
standard that replaces them. However, since these standards exist in
firmware (the hardware is interoperable), these modems are usually software upgradeable to the V.90 standard. However, unless the modem has
sufficient onboard flash memory (EEPROM) to hold the code for both its
original standard and the new V.90 standard, you may lose one when you
switch to the other. All of this is particularly important because of the long
shelf life of modems in stores and the future availability of bargains if you
don't mind taking a few minutes to do the firmware upgrade.

There are several limitations on what speed you can actually expect out of
your 56-Kb/s modem, not the least of these being the FCC, which limits
transmissions to 53 Kb/s by law. In order for you to reach 56 Kb/s on
downloads, you need to be dialing into an ISP or other source with a true
digital modem. In all point-to-point calls, the central telephone office,
where the calls are actually switched, stands in between. The phone com-
pany networks are all digital, allowing for clean, high-speed transfers
between switching points, and for 56 Kb/s to work, your ISP must be dig-
itally connected to that network. The 56-Kb/s modem in your PC is strictly an analog device, so an A/D conversion is done at the central office on

your upstream data, and a D/A conversion is done on your downstream data (downloads). As it happens, the line noise that limited modem speeds to 33 Kb/s is largely caused by A/D conversion, which is why your upstream speed is still limited to 33 Kb/s. Since the all-digital connection between the ISP and the central office eliminates the A/D conversion on the downstream link, speeds of up to 56 Kb/s become possible. However, if there are other noise sources involved, due to poor house-to-central-office wiring, you may never reach these speeds. In fact, if your current 28-Kb/s modem rarely connects at the full 28 Kb/s, you're going to be disappointed at 56 Kb/s as well.

One rather pointless controversy in the computer world centers around the choice of internal and external modems. External modems are about three times more expensive and require a separate AC power supply, an open serial port on the PC, and a serial cable to be connected. The benefits of external modems are that they are easily portable from one PC to another, and they are usually equipped with light-emitting diodes (LEDs), which can be used for troubleshooting. There was a time, maybe 10 years ago, when the benefits of external modems outweighed the costs, but that time is long gone. The choice that remains is whether to buy an internal modem that is 100 percent Plug and Play, or one that has jumpers or switches for hard-wiring the settings. In the long run, I've found that modems that offer a manual override to set a COM port and interrupt by jumpers or switches are useful if you add any additional adapters to your PC in the future.

Other Adapters

There are just too many permutations on sound cards and network adapters and speakers to cover them all in this book. Sound cards and speakers, if you're interested in the quality stuff, are continually reviewed in PC magazines and on Internet websites. Network adapters are pretty generic, and you'll pay a premium for brand and speed. All adapters you buy should be Plug and Play, which allows the computer to handle all of the resource configuration for you. None of the PCs built in this book require any manual configuration of adapters or resource planning.

Adapter/Option Type	Special Features	Basic Price	Purchasing Considerations
Cable modem	High-speed "always connected" Internet access	$200	Cable franchise must support digital services
56-Kb/s V.90 modem	Voice modem	$15 to $50	Backward support for k56flex or x2 if required by Internet service provider
16-bit sound	Game port	$15	Sound quality mediocre
PCI sound card	Wave table sound	$20 to $50	Better sound quality; aficionados check magazine product reviews
Speakers	AC power amplifier	$8 to $50	Wattage, subwoofer
10/100BaseT network adapter	Plug and Play	$10	Hub required
Network hub	Number of ports	$40 to $500	Twisted-pair cable and crimp tool required or buy premade cables
Assorted cables	Printer, USB, Ultra DMA	$2 to $10	Buy mail order; huge markup in retail stores

CHAPTER 3

Before You Assemble Your PC

The following checklist should be completed when you order PC parts to ensure that you have enough components to assemble a working PC.

☐	ATX case	(Including 250-watt or better power supply)
☐	ATX	(Slot A, Socket 370, Slot 1, Slot 2 or Super 7)
	motherboard	CPU (Slot A) AMD Athlon—also known as K7
		CPU (Socket 370) Pentium III FCPGA or Celeron PPGA
		CPU (Slot 1) Pentium III, Pentium II, or Celeron SECC
		CPU (Slot 2) Pentium III Xeon or Pentium II Xeon
		CPU (Super 7) AMD K6-3 or AMD K6-2
☐	RAM	32 MB (minimum) SDRAM for 66-MHz bus
		32 MB (minimum) PC-100 SDRAM for 100-MHz bus
		32 MB (minimum) PC-133 SDRAM for 133-MHz bus
☐	Video	AGP video adapter if motherboard lacks onboard video
☐	Floppy drive	1.44 MB 3.5-inch floppy drive
☐	Hard drive	8 GB IDE hard drive or larger
☐	CD or CDR	44X CD-ROM or CD recorder
	or DVD	2X or faster DVD (only if interested in viewing movies)
☐	Keyboard	Keyboard with PS/2-style connector
☐	Mouse	Mouse with PS/2-style connector
☐	Operating system	Windows Millennium, 2000, 98, or Linux

Optional but highly recommended*

☐	Modem	56-Kb/s V.90 modem
☐	Sound adapter	PCI sound card
☐	Network adapter	10/100BaseT network adapter
☐	Speakers	Speakers with separate power cord for amplifier

*All of the adapters may be included on a highly integrated motherboard.

Handling Parts and General Assembly Guidelines

Walking across a carpet can generate a static electric charge of 30,000 volts or more on your body. This is often manifested as a spark leaping from your hand to a doorknob or to another person, creating a shock you both can feel. That same discharge, harmless to people (and doorknobs) because of the minute amount of electrical current involved, can ruin expensive computer parts in a flash. Other activities that can generate static electricity include removing Styrofoam-encased parts from shipping boxes, peeling protective bubble wrap off drives, even sitting with your feet up on a chair rung and moving your arms about. That's the bad news.

The good news is that you can avoid building up a static electric charge, or at least zapping your computer components, by taking a few precautions. Most important, don't unpack your computer parts or assemble your PC in a room where you have recently received a static electric shock.

Next, get in the habit of frequently touching an electrical ground as you work. This could be a screw on the faceplate of an electrical outlet, a cold water pipe, or the metal case of any electrical appliance or tool that uses a three-prong plug. Also, make sure that the most sensitive (and expensive) components, such as the CPU, RAM, and motherboard, are never the first thing you touch after walking across the room or wrestling with some packaging. If you have a damp basement in your home, this is the ideal place to assemble your PC, because increased humidity lessens static electric discharges. If the neighborhood children flock to your home to chase each other around, sparks flying, you might consider the additional precaution of a grounding strap. Any decent electronics store will sell you a Velcro wristband with a coiled wire (as on a telephone handset) that can be clipped to a ground point, virtually guaranteeing that your body won't build up a potentially harmful charge.

The other primary danger to your computer components, other than dropping them on the floor, is the electricity generated by the computer power supply. Computers are often powered up with the case off when first assembled, either to make sure they work or because a configuration jumper requires an initial power-up before final placement. Even in the old days, before ATX power supplies, this was probably a bigger source of component damage than static electricity, as technicians and hobbyists alike would forget that the PC was turned on and proceed to add or remove an adapter. This can cause power spikes and short circuits, which can easily damage adapters and motherboards. Loose screws, fallen into the guts of the PC and forgotten or tumbling off their "temporary" storage place on the power supply or other surface, are probably the leading cause of short circuits. It's always a good idea to pick up your case and shake it gently from side to side while listening for stray screws before you plug the AC power cord into the power supply.

ATX power supplies and motherboards, although generally safer and easier to work with than the older AT standard they replace, create one new problem. With old power supplies, if the switch was off and the fan was quiet, it was safe to work on the PC. No current was flowing, and the power supply was intentionally left plugged into the wall so the case could provide an electrical ground. The new ATX power supplies, unless equipped with a override switch on the supply itself, are never really off. The motherboard is always receiving a trickle of current to power the on/off decision making and to afford the ability to "wake up" the computer to a preset alarm. In addition, to support network adapters and the modem's ability to wake up the PC for incoming traffic, a 720-mA current must be present on the 5-V supply to the bus adapters. This means that you should never work on your ATX PC with the power supply plugged into the wall. Some people might prefer to disconnect the power supply from the motherboard while working on the PC, but these connectors aren't designed to be made up a large number of times, and the step could easily be forgotten. Finally, most power supplies are equipped with a 115/230-V switch right below the socket for the cord to the wall outlet. Power supplies sold in the United States are set to 115 V, but it doesn't hurt to double-check.

The only tool you absolutely need to assemble a PC is a Phillips screwdriver. A regular screwdriver is sometimes handy for prying, if prying is called for, and the small brass standoffs that hold the motherboard in place may be tightened with pliers or a nutdriver. A large work area isn't necessary; room for your case (on its side if a tower type), with space alongside to lay out your motherboard and parts, is sufficient. The area must be well lit, and a ground point, as discussed previously, should be available.

Before you begin to assemble your PC, look through the pictures to become familiar with the steps involved. You should also leaf through the photographs for the systems you aren't building, particularly the steps for installing drives and connecting peripherals. The photography for the other systems may be more illustrative in these steps because of the different case geometry or a less congested port area. Next, consult the documentation enclosed with the parts you have purchased to see what variations there are. In all cases, the instructions that come with your parts supersede the instructions given in this book. For example, there is no standard for configuring a motherboard to work with a particular brand and speed of CPU. The jumper or switch settings used must be taken from your motherboard manual or from the website of your motherboard manufacturer.

The PCs we will build in this book were chosen to be representative of the majority of options you may encounter. The first is a minitower system with a highly integrated motherboard that supports both Slot 1 and Socket 370 CPUs. This system will be built in two options: a Slot 1 Pentium III and a Socket 370 Celeron. The second system is an Athlon (also known as K7) Slot A system in a midtower case. Third is a midtower Slot 1 system built as both a Pentium II and a Celeron SECC. Last comes Socket 7 motherboard with a K6 series CPU in a desktop case.

	Chapter 4	**Chapter 5**	**Chapter 6**	**Chapter 7**
Case type	Minitower	Midtower	Midtower	Desktop
CPU type(s) used in build	Pentium III/Celeron	Athlon (K7)	Pentium II/Celeron	K6
Motherboard features	Slot 1 and Socket 370, integrated AGP video, sound, 10BaseT network, 56-Kb/s modem	Slot A, onboard sound, dual CPU fan, CPU speed and voltage autodetect	Slot 1, onboard sound, Intel 440 LX chipset (66-MHz bus)	Socket 7, supports AMD K6 series, Cyrix M2, Intel Pentium MMX
RAM installed	64-MB PC-133 (1 DIMM)	256-MB PC-100 (2 DIMMs)	64-MB SDRAM (2 DIMMs)	64-MB SDRAM (2 DIMMs)
Highlights	Adapter extenders, easy-out power supply, Slot 1 and Socket 370 CPU mounting	16-GB UDMA/66 hard drive, second drive, second case fan, detailed drive cabling	Removable motherboard pan, front panel removal, clear adapter mounting	Removable 3.5-inch drive cage, rail-mounted CD ROM, detailed peripheral connections

Problems to Watch Out For

There are five basic things that can go wrong when assembling a PC that will prevent it from powering up or operating properly:

1. **Faulty connections**—This is the most common problem, and it includes improperly made ribbon cable connections to the drives or motherboard; switch, fan, and other small connections made to wrong points on motherboard; partially made power connections; poorly seated CPUs and DIMMs; and adapter cards partially out of slots. These are illustrated in detail after this discussion.

2. **Improper settings**—These can be jumpers or switches on the motherboard, the voltage switch on the power supply, or software settings made in CMOS setup after initial power-up. The wrong voltage selection on the power supply (115 V/230 V) will damage components, as can an improper CPU voltage or speed setting on some motherboards. Improper software settings will generally result in slower or inconsistent operation (lockups). In all instances, the only source for motherboard settings is the small motherboard manual that comes with the motherboard. Most new motherboards can automatically detect all settings and are sold with this option selected, but always check the manual.

3. **D.O.A. (Dead On Arrival) parts**—Although this problem is less common than generally thought, especially given the poor packaging used by many mail-order vendors and incredibly low component prices, you may encounter a D.O.A. component. Troubleshooting which component is dead almost necessitates access to a working PC to swap out parts. This is a major reason to buy at least your motherboard, case, CPU, RAM, and video adapter (the minimum needed to get a "live" screen) from the same vendor to simplify return issues.

4. **Incompatible or poorly selected parts**—This is rare with motivated do-it-yourselfers, but a careless selection of parts from an Internet site may leave you with an 800-MHz CPU and a motherboard that only goes to 550 MHz, or even a high-performance AGP adapter and a motherboard with built-in video and no AGP slot. The best way to avoid these problems is to keep a written list of the parts you are ordering and not make snap decisions on attractive components.

5. **Carelessness**—Dropping parts, leaving loose screws rattling around the case, wearing a wool sweater and pulling it off over your head just before unpacking the RAM without grounding yourself first—all of these things happen. The only antidote for carelessness is staying awake, but not by drinking a coffee over your open PC!

Faulty Connections

Probably the most common mistake of new PC builders is not making sure the adapter cards are properly seated in the slots before closing up the case. Even if an adapter seats properly when you initially push it into the slot, it may pop partially out when nearby adapters are inserted. Paradoxically, the leading reason for PCI and AGP adapters to pop out of the slot is the insertion of the screw that is intended to secure them. This happens because the PCI slots, and even more so the AGP slot, are located further from the back of the case where the screw is inserted than the older ISA slots. When the screw forces down the port end of the adapter, the adapter may pivot on the back edge of the slot holder, causing the front edge to lever out of contact. This is illustrated in Figure 3.1.

A similar result often occurs when memory DIMMs are inserted unevenly. This is the reason we emphasize seating the DIMM with two thumbs, and letting the white locking levers at the ends of the DIMM slots raise into place as the DIMM is properly seated. Wedging the DIMM in on one side first to get it started and pulling up on the locking levers to encourage it can result in the failed insertion illustrated in Figure 3.2. The levers do pull up, even the though the DIMM is barely halfway in.

Figure 3.1

PCI adapter partially seated in the slot.

The most likely reason for a system to fail to power up once it's plugged in and the switch is pressed on the front panel is that the power switch lead is attached to the motherboard improperly. This can result from misreading the motherboard manual or markings on the motherboard, but it also occurs simply because the connection blocks for panel leads are highly compact. Squinting through a maze of wires in a poorly lit work area can lead to all sorts of missed connections. The power switch, a two-lead connector, is shown in Figure 3.3 with only one half of the connector on the posts. On newer power supplies, don't forget to check the override switch on the back of the supply.

Figure 3.2

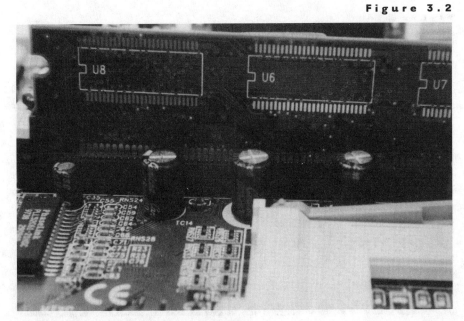

DIMM improperly seated in the socket.

Figure 3.3

Power switch missed connection.

All of the newer CPU types used in PCs are keyed so they can only be inserted in one orientation, but all of them can fail through partial insertion. This is more common with the slot-type CPUs such as the Athlon for Slot A and the Pentium III for Slot 1, because the edge connectors rely on spring force to make good contact with the processor cartridges, and therefore often require strong pressure to insert and seat properly. Normally, when a slot-type system is powered up with a partially seated CPU, the power LED comes on and the drives whir, but the system does nothing. Socket 370 and Socket 7 CPUs can also be partially inserted, usually due

Figure 3.4

Socket 7 CPU unevenly seated in the socket.

to being pushed into place with the locking lever only partially open. The lever can be closed with the CPU cocked on an angle, and the heat sink can even be locked into place over it.

The most problematic drive connection is always the floppy drive. The connectors on the drives are only rarely keyed, or even boxed, so the ribbon cable can go on backwards, missing one full row of the two rows of pins, or missing one column of pins at one end or another. Some floppy cabling problems are immediately apparent, because the small LED on the faceplate of the drive comes on and stays on permanently once the system is powered up. When any floppy drive problems are encountered, undo and remake the connection, removing the drive to get a good look if that's required. The hardest cabling problem to spot is the case of the two pins on the end missing the connector, which bends them a little as it is pushed on. When the cable is removed, the pins will still look straight as you sight down the drive, and the connection will continue to mate improperly until you bend them back.

The ribbon cables themselves are also prone to failure when removed and reinserted several times. This is due to the lack of a large rigid plastic header on the cable, which forces you to pull on the ribbon cable itself in some instances. If the stress relief breaks, the press-together connector will begin to open, and the spade contacts can separate from the cable.

Figure 3.5

Two pins missing the floppy ribbon cable.

Figure 3.6

Failed connector on the ribbon cable.

One last problem, although not a connector issue, is using the wrong screws in the wrong places. This simple mechanical issue can lead to stripped threads and endless frustration in trying to remove the screws at a later time. Coarse-thread screws are used for hard drives, case covers,

Figure 3.7

Fine- and coarse-thread screws.

and power supplies, and usually for adapter hold-down and motherboard mounting also. Fine-thread screws are generally only used with floppy drives and CD-ROM drives.

CHAPTER 4

Building a Pentium III or Celeron in a Minitower Case

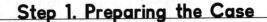

Step 1. Preparing the Case

This minitower case is an innovative design that offers both benefits and drawbacks. Part of the reason for choosing this case was variety, since we will illustrate two midtower builds with the Athlon and the Pentium II/Celeron systems, and a build in a desktop case with our Socket 7 system. The unique feature of this case is the power supply, which is latched into position and secured with one thumb screw. The case is somewhat cramped to work in, but it results in a compact system and is a good match for the highly integrated motherboard we chose.

Another feature of this case that you won't see in our older ATX systems is a punch-out I/O core cover located directly under the power supply. Also, like most new designs, the case cover consists of three separate lids, rather than one piece. Once the system is assembled, the motherboard can be accessed by removing two screws on "up" side, rather than a whole cover. Although the minitower is obviously designed to stand up, we work on it lying on one side, in the position where the I/O core is at the bottom. Begin by removing the side lids, each of which is held by two screws in the back of the case.

Figure 4.1

New minitower from rear.

The lid is slid straight back about a half an inch, to disengage the metal tongues from the edges of the case, then lifted straight up. When building a minitower without a hinged power supply, proceed to remove the motherboard pan at this point, as in the Pentium II build in Chapter 6. However, since the power supply can be removed entirely and there is no blocking support, we will be able to install the motherboard directly into the case..

Remove the box or bag with the spare parts and accessories from the case, and install the plastic or rubber feet on the case bottom that will keep the case from scratching the table or floor.

Figure 4.2

Case with the top lid off.

Step 2. Mounting Memory on the Motherboard

In Figure 4.3, the motherboard is removed from a static-proof bag and laid on a hard, flat surface on top of the thin nonconductive foam it came with. The three long black sockets with the white locking levers on each end to the lower right are the DIMM sockets. The motherboard chosen is one of the most highly integrated motherboards available, including sound, AGP

Figure 4.3

Motherboard fresh out of the box.

video, a 56-Kb/s modem, a 10/100BaseT network adapter, and the option to install either Slot 1 or Socket 370 Intel processors.

The single 64-MB DIMM is installed by aligning the notches in the bottom edge of the DIMM with the notches in the DIMM socket. As with most motherboard designs, the first (or only) DIMM installed in the system must be placed in first bank, labeled "DIMM 1" on this motherboard. The white levers to either side of the socket must be spread before you attempt to insert the DIMM.

Push evenly on the DIMM with a thumb on both ends. The locking levers should slowly draw in until the DIMM is firmly seated. Sometimes, a little wiggling and some heavy pressure is needed, but you should never dig one end of the DIMM into the socket first and try to force down the other end after it.

F i g u r e   4 . 4

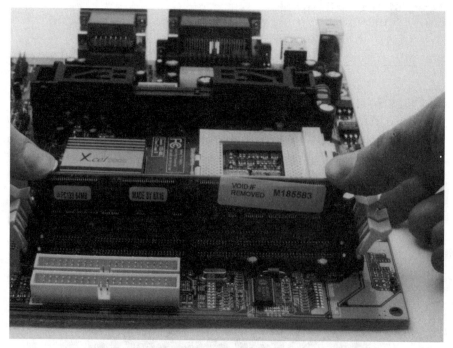

Seating the DIMM with even pressure.

When the DIMM is seated in the socket, check that the white locking levers are fully engaged. When the PC is powered on for the first time and you enter CMOS setup to set the CPU speed, you should also make sure that PC-133 memory is set to a speed of 6 n and PC-100 DIMM is set to 8 n. Otherwise, they will run at a slower default. Since only one memory speed setting is possible for the system, avoid mixing modules of different speeds in a system.

Step 3a. Pentium III Option

The first step with such a flexible motherboard is to select the CPU package being installed with a jumper right next to the sockets, as detailed in the manual that comes with the motherboard. For variety, we will install a Pentium III in Slot 1, and then as a variant path, a Celeron in Socket 370.

Figure 4.5

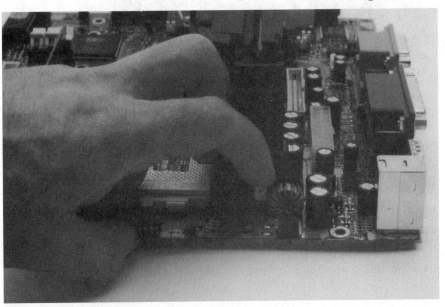

Setting the jumper to Slot 1.

Next, raise the folded Slot 1 supports that will receive the Pentium III. On many Slot 1 motherboards, the supports are supplied separately and must be snapped into or screwed to the motherboard.

Figure 4.6

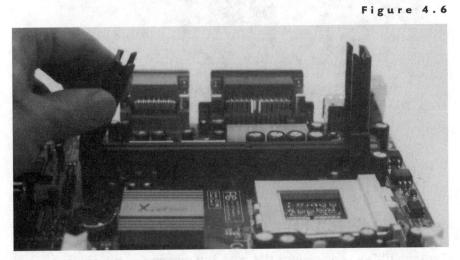

Raising the Slot 1 supports.

This Pentium III processor is a single-edge contact cartridge 2 (S.E.C.C 2) for Slot 1 motherboards. Both the Pentium III and the motherboard are capable of a 100-MHz front side bus, and newer versions of the Pentium III are capable of 133-MHz bus operation.

F i g u r e   4 . 7

Pentium III.

We have actually disassembled the Pentium III fan and heat sink to illustrate that the fan is a replaceable unit. Almost all Pentium III processors are sold with the heat sink and fan already installed, primarily to reduce the chances a customer will damage the cartridge mounting these snap-together units, or attempt to use it without an active cooling device.

F i g u r e   4 . 8

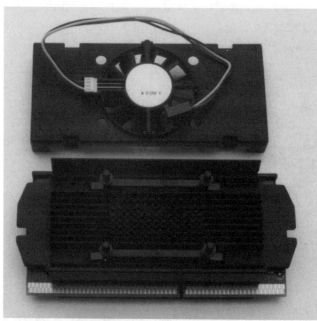

Pentium III from back—heat sink with fan removed.

The fan assembly snaps over the four plastic posts projecting from the heat sink. When plugged into the proper fan power point on the motherboard, the fan can be turned off and on as required. The power supply in this minitower also has a grille on the bottom of the case to draw hot air from away from the processor.

Figure 4.9

Pentium III—snapping fan onto heat sink.

As with the previously installed DIMM module, the edge of the connector on the Pentium III has a notch to one side that matches a key in the socket. Double-check that you are lowering the Pentium III in the right orientation, because it can take a good deal of pressure to properly mate a Slot 1 connector.

Figure 4.10

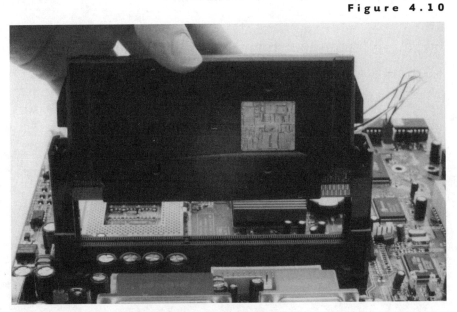

Lowering the Pentium III processor into Slot 1.

If your Pentium III package is equipped with compressible tabs on either end, hold these in while lowering the processor into the slot. Otherwise, push with a thumb on either end of the Pentium III, just like with the DIMM module, until you feel the Pentium III settle into place. The most common reason for a new Slot 1 system to fail to boot is a processor that isn't seated all the way.

Check the motherboard manual to see which of the several fan connection points on the motherboard is for the heat sink fan. This is commonly the fan1 connector, but it is found in a different place on every motherboard.

Figure 4.11

Connecting the heat sink fan to the motherboard.

Using the same motherboard, we will install a Socket 370 Celeron processor. As with the Pentium III, the first step is to select which CPU mounting will be used. In this case, move the jumper to the Socket 370 position.

Figure 4.12

Setting the jumper for Socket 370.

The Celeron package for Socket 370 is very similar in appearance to the old Socket 7 design, but the two are mutually incompatible. The PPGA (plastic pin grid array) packages for Socket 370 are lacking the corner pin on two corners, as opposed to one corner for Socket 7 chips.

Figure 4.13

Celeron processor for Socket 370.

The Celeron cannot be installed in a Socket 370 incorrectly because of the two keyed corners. The first step to installing the Celeron is to lift the locking lever at the side of the socket all the way up to the vertical position. Then, match up the corners of the chip to the socket and lower it directly into place.

Figure 4.14

Checking for proper Celeron alignment with the locking lever up.

The Celeron must seat perfectly flat in the socket. If it doesn't seem to want to sit all the way down, double-check that the locking lever is all the way up and that it didn't start in cocked to one side. Once the Celeron is seated properly, the lever action may be fairly stiff as you lock it in place. The lever must return all the way to the tuck position alongside the socket.

Figure 4.15

Heat sink with fan.

The heat sink and fan for Socket 370 processors are locked over the Celeron to the socket, not the Celeron itself. The same heat sink and fan can be used for any Socket 370 processor.

The first step to install the heat sink is to slide the steel spring all the way to one side, then hook that side over the back of the plastic projection on the Socket 370 base.

Figure 4.16

Hooking the spring onto the back of the base.

Figure 4.17

The next step is to slide the heat sink back down the spring, so that it aligns with the edge of the Celeron. Then, lower the heat sink assembly over the Celeron, keeping the heat sink squarely over the chip.

Lowering the heat sink over the Celeron.

When the heat sink is flat over the socket and squarely over the chip, push the spring down over the plastic ear on the front of the socket. It's best to do this with one finger while firmly holding the heat sink assembly in place with your hand.

Figure 4.18

Locking the heat sink in place.

After the heat sink is installed, the fan lead is connected to the fan1 power point. While you have the motherboard manual open to find the fan1 connector, it's a good time to familiarize yourself with the other connectors on the motherboard, because once it is installed in the case, you may find your view of these partially obstructed by other components.

Figure 4.19

Connecting to power fan.

Step 4. Mounting the Motherboard

The instructions for mounting the motherboard and assembling the rest of the system are identical with either the Pentium III or the Celeron in place. The first step with this particular case design is to remove the power supply to gain access to the motherboard pan. The power supply is held in by a single thumb-screw with a large plastic head, which is removed by hand.

Figure 4.20

Removing the power supply thumbscrew.

The power supply now hinges up on the back of the case and is lifted out. The geometry of this case almost necessitates this "easy out" feature, because the power supply, when installed, blocks access to the floppy cable, to the CPU, and even to the power supply connection to the motherboard!

Now, place the motherboard in the case to check which punch-outs in the I/O core must be removed. Most motherboards ship with a foil I/O shield, which exactly matches the motherboard I/O core and fits in the standard ATX I/O opening (see the Pentium II midtower system for a good illustration of this). This case comes with a standard shield installed that has punch-outs that can be removed to match the motherboard I/O core.

Figure 4.21

Fitting the motherboard in the case to check I/O core alignment.

After noting which punch-outs need to be removed, take the motherboard back out. While pushing with a Phillips screwdriver or other reasonably blunt instrument to break the punch-outs free, use your other hand to hold the I/O shield from the back so it doesn't get bent out of shape. However, make sure that your hand doesn't end up behind the punch-out, because even a blunt screwdriver will hurt if you stab it into your hand.

Now comes the tricky part. Place the motherboard back in the case, and check that the I/O core matches up with the shield, so that the motherboard is resting in its final position. Now look for the holes in the mother-

Figure 4.22

Punching out a blank for the sound connections.

board where you will be placing screws to secure it in the case. These holes are ringed by silvery solder. Try to remember where a couple of holes near one side of the motherboard are, then move it out of the way just enough to reveal the holes in the motherboard pan where the standoffs, or screw receptacles, will be installed. After you get the standoffs on one side in, you'll have to remove the motherboard each time you line up new holes, because you don't want to drag it on the standoffs you've installed. The type of standoffs supplied with the case varies with the manufacturer, so look at the other systems in this book if the standoffs used here don't match yours.

Figure 4.23

Inserting a standoff in the motherboard pan.

Spring steel standoffs can be inserted without any tools by gently squeezing them and putting them in place. Avoid using pliers or squeezing too hard, because the steel will stay bent and the standoff will rattle around until you get a screw in it. Use as many standoffs as will match holes in your motherboard and pan—six in most cases.

Finally, the motherboard is installed in the case for good. Double-check the I/O core to make sure that all the ports on the motherboard are accessible. With a good light or flashlight, look through the mounting holes in the motherboard and make sure that you can see the edges of all the standoffs you inserted before you start installing screws.

Figure 4.24

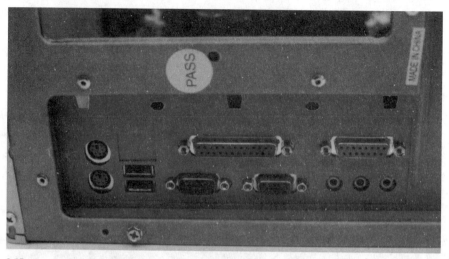

I/O core matched through the case back.

Now begin putting screws in the motherboard, but don't tighten them until all of the screws are installed. If the number of screws used doesn't match the number of standoffs you put in, take it out again and remove the standoff that didn't line up.

Figure 4.25

Screwing in the motherboard.

Step 5. Making Connections and Reinstalling Power Supply

Check for any other connection points that will be obstructed when the power supply is installed. It is found that with this motherboard, the floppy drive connector will end up under the power supply. On checking the motherboard manual for the proper cable orientation, we also find that the pin 1 orientation of the floppy connector is the reverse of the IDE connectors! This is rare for motherboards, which generally keep all connections oriented the same way, and it goes to show that you should always check the manual.

Figure 4.26

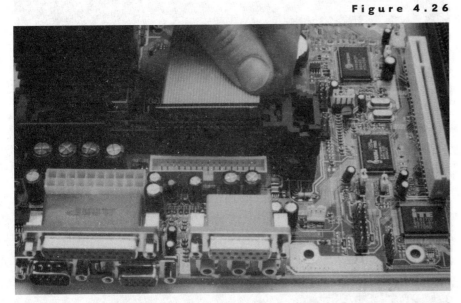

Attaching the floppy cable with red wire keyed to pin 1.

The ATX power supply connector consists of 20 wires in a single snap-on unit and is keyed to fit one way only. Since the connection point on the motherboard ends up under the power supply itself, it's necessary to make this connection before putting the power supply back in.

Before reinstalling the power supply, check that the 115/230 V switch located on the back of the supply is on the correct voltage for your country. This is 115 V in the U.S. and 230 V in most other countries, but if you aren't sure, find out.

Figure 4.27

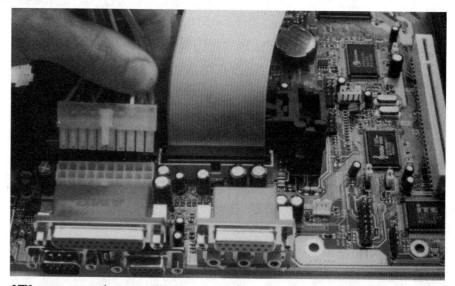

ATX power supply connection.

Return the power supply to the case, hinging it over the top edge, then lowering it into position. Put the thumb screw back in immediately afterwards so it doesn't get forgotten.

Figure 4.28

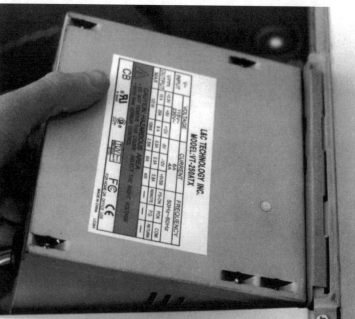
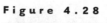

Reinstalling the power supply.

Step 6. Installing the Adapter Extension Brackets

Almost all PCs will be built with at least one add-on adapter, but this motherboard is an exception. All of the basic adapter functions are onboard: AGP video, 56-Kb/s modem, 10/100BaseT network adapter, and full sound capability. However, the standard I/O core doesn't provide enough room to accommodate the network and modem ports, so the motherboard manufacturer provides adapter extension brackets that are little more than a slot plate with a port, although a small circuit card is included.

Figure 4.29

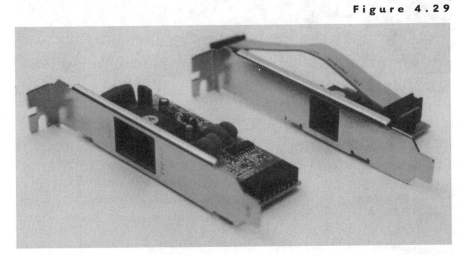

Adapter extension brackets.

The adapter extender is screwed into place on the back rail. Always screw in any adapters or adapter extenders immediately after you install them, making sure that the port opening is fully exposed through the slot.

The network adapter is then connected to the motherboard by way of a small ribbon cable connection, which is kept short to reduce electrical noise. This requires that the adapter be mounted in the slot nearest to the connection point. The ribbon cable is keyed with a red wire that must be connected to the pin 1 end of the connector.

The modem extender on this motherboard is really a somewhat unique design. Rather than wasting a cable, the adapter extender is plugged directly onto the motherboard to a proprietary connection block that leaves no chance for backward connections.

Figure 4.30

Connecting the network adapter extension cable.

Seat the modem firmly, making sure that it settles over both rows of pins, then install the screw. With all the integrated features on a motherboard like this, you don't need to buy or install any conventional adapters at all. However, if we did want to add more functionality to this system, there is only one shared ISA/PCI slot available.

Figure 4.31

Securing the modem.

When the system is built with the Slot 1 Pentium III option, you can see what a tight fit the cabling is. Both the floppy cable and the power connector would have been impossible to install without first removing the power supply. While the combination of a cramped case and a crowded motherboard may not be ideal, you only have to put it together once. It does provide an excellent illustration of why you must always be thinking ahead to the next step, and why you should look over all the systems in this book to see what you may encounter.

Figure 4.32

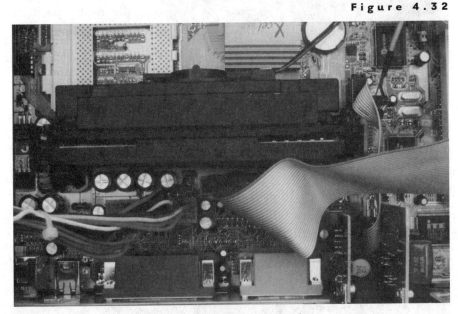

Pentium III with motherboard connections made.

Step 7. Installing Drives

There are two connectors on a floppy drive and no jumpers you need to set. However, it is important to closely examine the drive before installing it in the case to note which is the pin 1 end of the connector. Unlike hard drives and CD drives, floppy connectors are rarely built to accept keyed connectors, and when they are, they are occasionally keyed the wrong way.

Figure 4.33

Rear of the floppy drive.

Remove the plastic blank from the front of the case where you will install the floppy drive by popping it out with your fingers from behind. Then slide the drive through in the upright position from the front of the case. Normally, we would preinstall the ribbon cable on the drive to avoid mistakes, but since the ribbon cable connection to the motherboard is so awkward in this system, we do it with the drive installed.

Secure the floppy drive with four screws as soon as you install it. It's much easier to install the cables with the drive solidly fixed in place so it does not yield when you push to make connections.

Figure 4.34

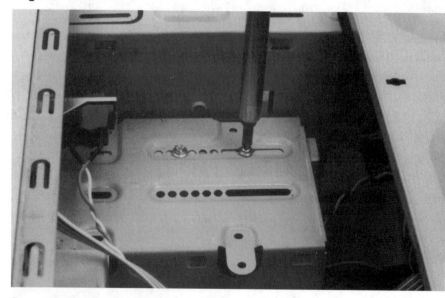

Securing the floppy drive.

The ribbon cable goes on with the red key wire at the pin 1 end of the connector. Sometimes the drive connector is only labeled with a "33" or "34", which tells you that pin 1 is on the opposite end. It's crucial to get the connector on without missing an entire row of pins, or bending two out of the way at one end or the other. About 99 percent of the instances of floppy drives not working in new systems are due to the ribbon cable being pushed on wrong.

Figure 4.35

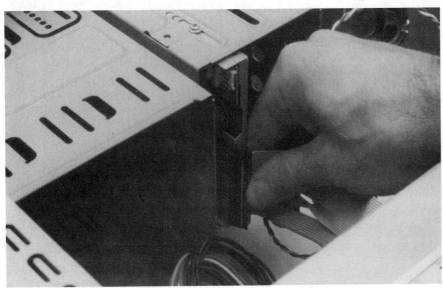

Installing the ribbon cable.

The power connector to the floppy drive is seated with the shallow cutout on the back of the small connector from the power supply seated over the plastic tab that extends over the four pins on the drive, or down toward the circuit board if the plastic tab is absent.

Figure 4.36

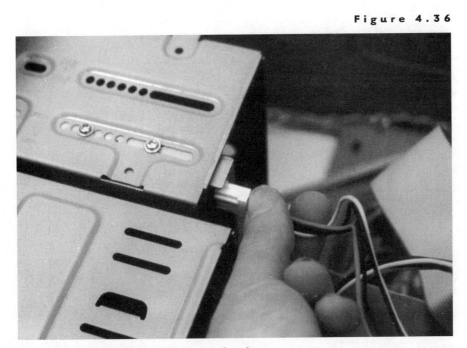

Installing the floppy-drive power lead.

The 20-GB IDE Western
Digital hard drive chosen
is a mid-range drive, good
capacity with reasonable
speed at a 5400 rpm spin-
dle speed. The same basic
Caviar drive is available
with more cache and a
7200 rpm spindle speed
for around $20 more.
All of the information
required to install the
drive is contained in the
informative label on the
cover.

Figure 4.37

Western Digital Caviar 205AA.

The first step to installing the hard drive into our system is to set the drive
select jumper to "Master." The CDR will be set to "Slave" and installed on
the same ribbon cable.

Figure 4.38

Setting the jumper to "Master."

The hard drive is installed from the inside of the case, in the 3.5-inch bay under the floppy drive. Line the drive up in a position where it can be secured with four screws. If the fit seems too tight as you try to slide the drive in, loosen the screws holding the floppy drive until it slides in easily. Do not put the drive in on an angle and try to straighten it in place.

Secure the drive with four screws, two on each side, making sure that the drive is level with the bottom of the cage. Retighten any screws you may have loosened in the floppy drive.

Figure 4.39

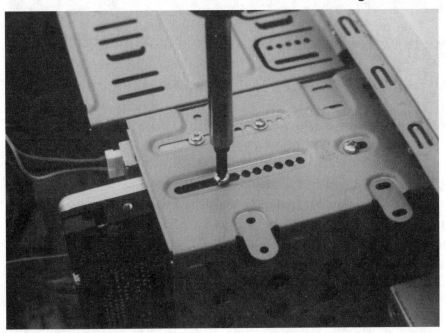

Securing the hard drive.

The hard drive ribbon cable is installed with the red wire in the connector keyed to pin 1. Most production hard drives orient the connector with pin 1 toward the power connector.

Figure 4.40

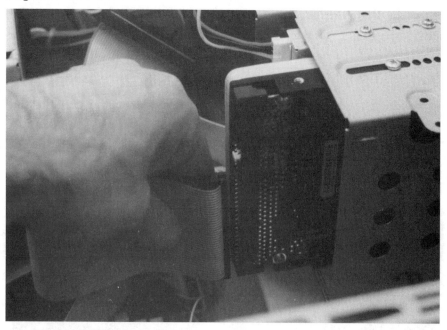

Installing the IDE ribbon cable.

Hard drives are designed with a power connection socket that is keyed to the large connectors on the power supply leads by angling two corners of the socket so the connection can only be made one way. Take a good look at the connector and socket to identify the angled corners before mating the connection. The connector should push into the socket at least a quarter of an inch, which often requires strong pressure.

Figure 4.41

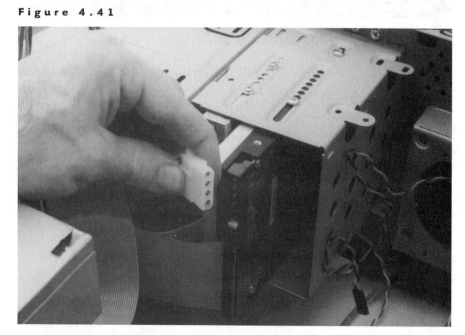

Installing the hard drive power lead.

As an IDE device, our CDR is equipped with a master/slave jumper, just like the hard drive. Since we will be sharing an IDE cable between the two drives, and the hard drive is set to "Master," we set the CDR to "Slave" before installing the drive. Along with the IDE ribbon cable and the power lead, all CD drives have a connector for stereo sound that is active when you play a music CD in the drive. The thin cable may be labeled or keyed for keeping the left and right stereo channels straight, though if you get it backwards, it doesn't hurt anything. New drives usually sport a two-pin connection for digital audio, as do most new sound cards or sound-enabled motherboards, but this connection is only required if you want to record digital music directly from a CD, which is usually a violation of somebody's copyright.

Figure 4.42

Installing the "Slave" jumper on the CDR drive with cables connected for illustration.

The plastic cover for the top bay in the minitower case is popped out from behind with the fingers. The drive can be installed in any of the 5.25-inch bays, but the top bay lacks the metal RF shield that covers the lower two bays, so it's most convenient to fill it first. The drive is then slid in from the front of the case. See the desktop K6 series system for an example of mounting a CD drive with a rail assembly.

Secure the drive with four screws and connect the shared ribbon cable with the red wire on pin 1, then insert the keyed power lead. Connect the IDE ribbon cable to the primary IDE controller port on the motherboard. Check the motherboard manual for the orientation of pin 1 on the connector to match the red key wire in the ribbon, unless it is clearly marked on the board. Some motherboards ship with keyed IDE ribbon cables that have a special locking mechanism on the motherboard end, so the choice is made for you.

Figure 4.43

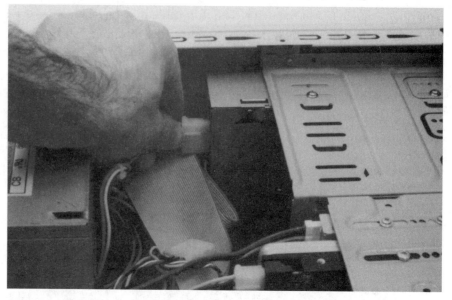

Connecting the CDR power lead.

Make the stereo sound connection to the motherboard, which integrates the sound adapter functions. The motherboard offers two different CD sound connectors to accommodate both cable types currently in use.

Figure 4.44

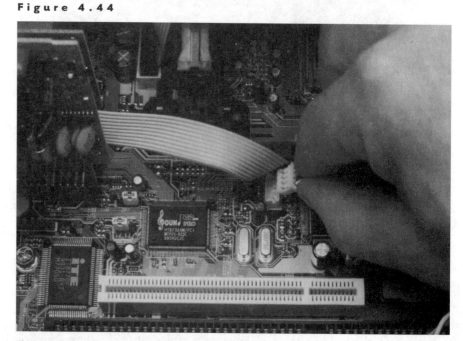

Connecting CD stereo to the motherboard.

Step 8. Finishing Up and Closing the Case

The last step is normally to make the front panel connections to the motherboard. These include case speaker, reset switch, power switch, power, and hard drive LEDs. You need to have the motherboard manual open for this procedure because the motherboard connector block is rarely labeled. If you find you have an LED that doesn't light when the build is complete, the connector for that LED is probably on backwards.

Figure 4.45

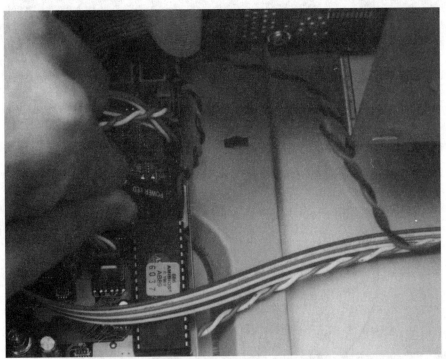

Connecting the front-panel leads.

Lift the whole case off the table and gently shake it back and forth, listening for loose screws or other forgotten bits. Next, replace the bottom lid and screw it into place. If you have a clean work area and a monitor available, you may want to stand the case up and skip replacing the top lid until you turn the system on and see that all of your connections were made correctly.

Check the voltage switch one more time, and plug in the power supply. If the supply is equipped with an override power switch as this supply is, turn that switch on. When working on this system in the future, the switch can be turned off, rather than disconnecting the power cord as in other ATX systems.

Figure 4.46

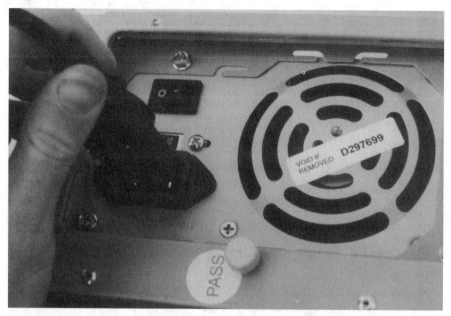

Plugging in the power supply and turning override switch on.

Now connect the power supply, keyboard, mouse, video, and speakers if you have them. We show the keyboard and mouse connectors here; see the midtower and desktop systems for making the other connections.

Figure 4.47

Connecting the keyboard and mouse.

The first time you power up your new PC, you will have to enter CMOS setup to set the CPU and memory bus speed. This is usually accomplished by hitting the Delete key as soon as the first text appears on the screen, or by following on screen instructions to enter CMOS, such as "Hit <F1> to enter Setup."

Figure 4.48

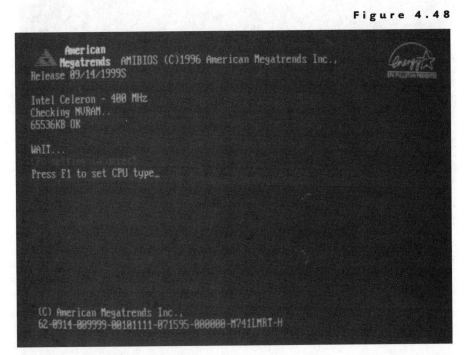

The screen on initial power-up.

The first task on entering CMOS setup is to set the CPU speed. The main setup screen is navigated using the arrow keys. Go immediately to CPU Settings and hit Enter.

Figure 4.49

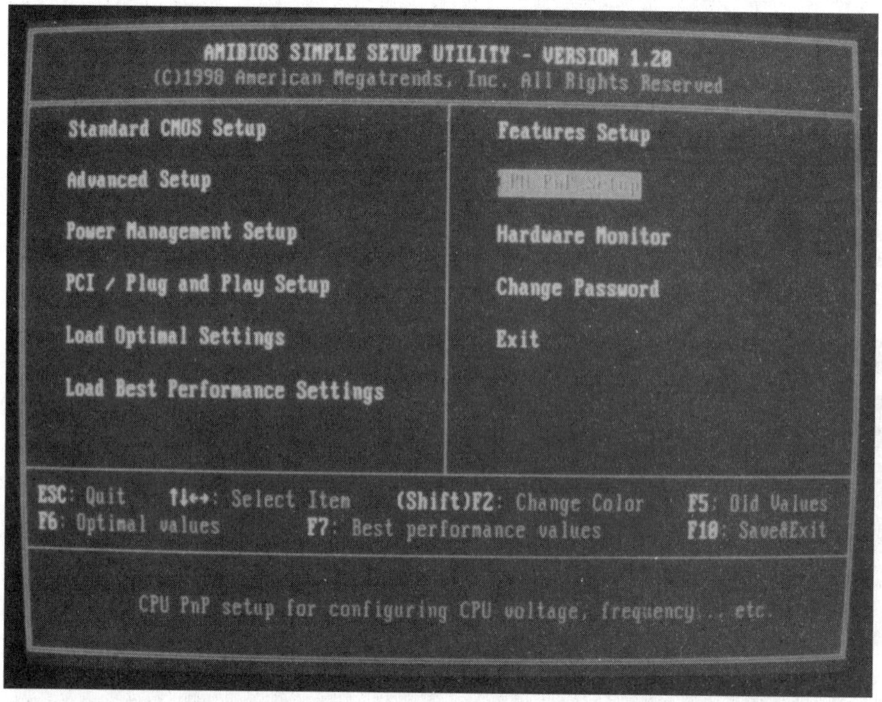

The main setup screen.

The system powers up for the first time at the lowest-speed settings for universal compatibility. The Pentium III processor used here is a 500-MHz CPU with a 100-MHz front-side bus. First change the "CPU core frequency,"

Figure 4.50

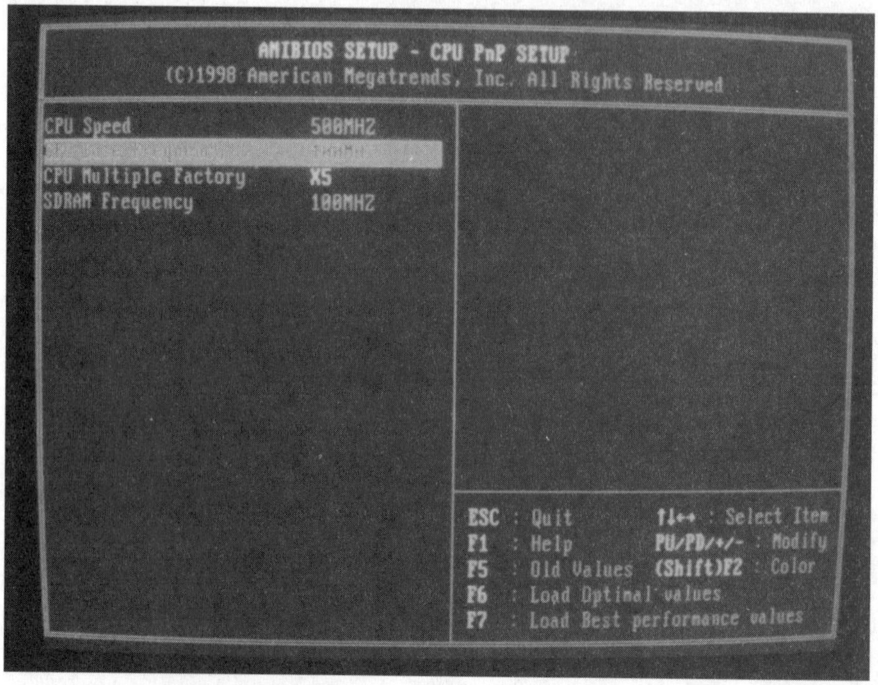

Setting the Pentium III speed.

which fixes the bus speed from the default 66 MHz to 100 MHz, by using the Page Up and Page Down or + and − keys, as given in the on-screen instructions at the lower right. Next, change the multiplier until the CPU speed reaches 500 MHz, which requires a multiplier of 5X.

For our Celeron build, leave the CPU Core Frequency on the default 66 MHz, and select the multiplier, 6X, which gives the 400-MHz CPU speed.

Figure 4.51

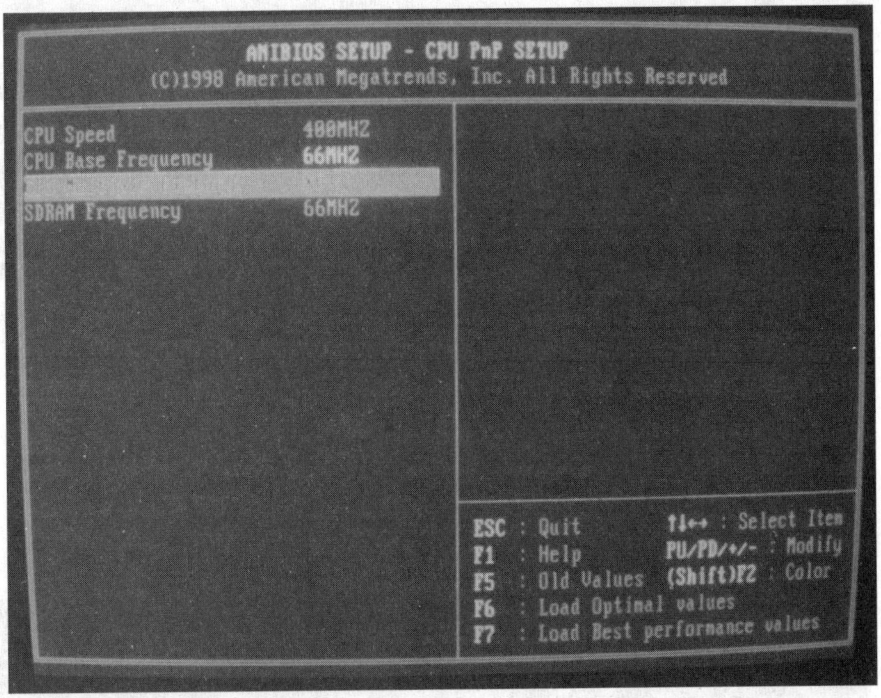

Setting the Celeron speed.

In either case, return to the main setup screen and go into Advanced Settings, where the speed of the SDRAM is set to 6 nS, since PC-133 memory is installed. Neither of the processors installed can take full advantage of the PC-133 module, designed to run on a 133-MHz front-side bus, but when there is no difference in module cost, it makes no sense to buy the slower parts.

The final step is to exit CMOS and save the new settings. At this point the PC is completely built, and the rest of the job is software installation. You do not need to set the drive types in CMOS setup as with older PCs. A 1.44-MB floppy drive for A: is the default, and the IDE drives are automatically detected and configured. With a new motherboard such as this one, you don't even need to tell it to boot to the CD-ROM your operating system will be installed from. The motherboard will check all of the drives for a bootable disk without being told.

Figure 4.52

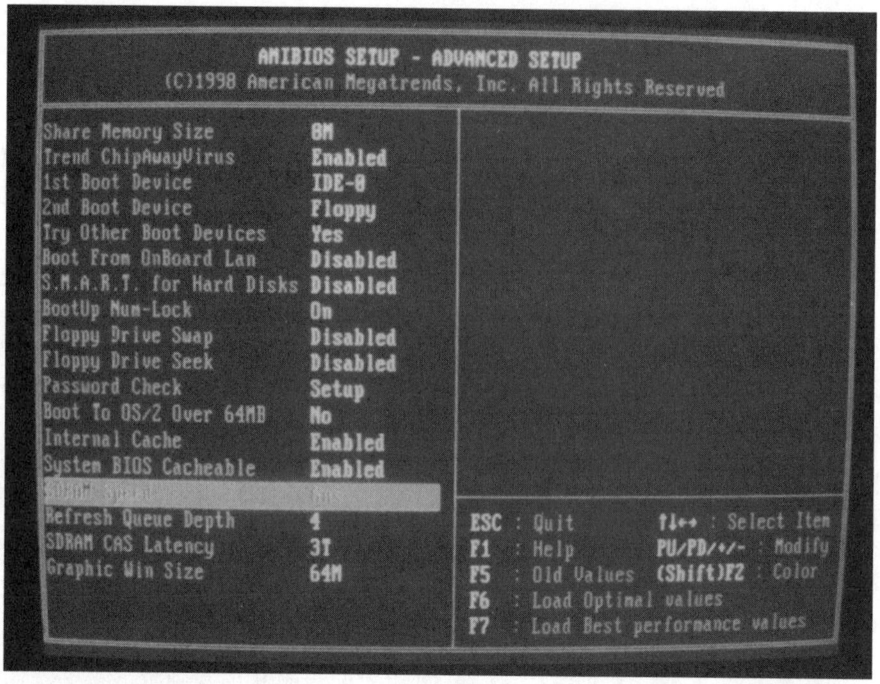

Setting the SDRAM speed.

Figure 4.53

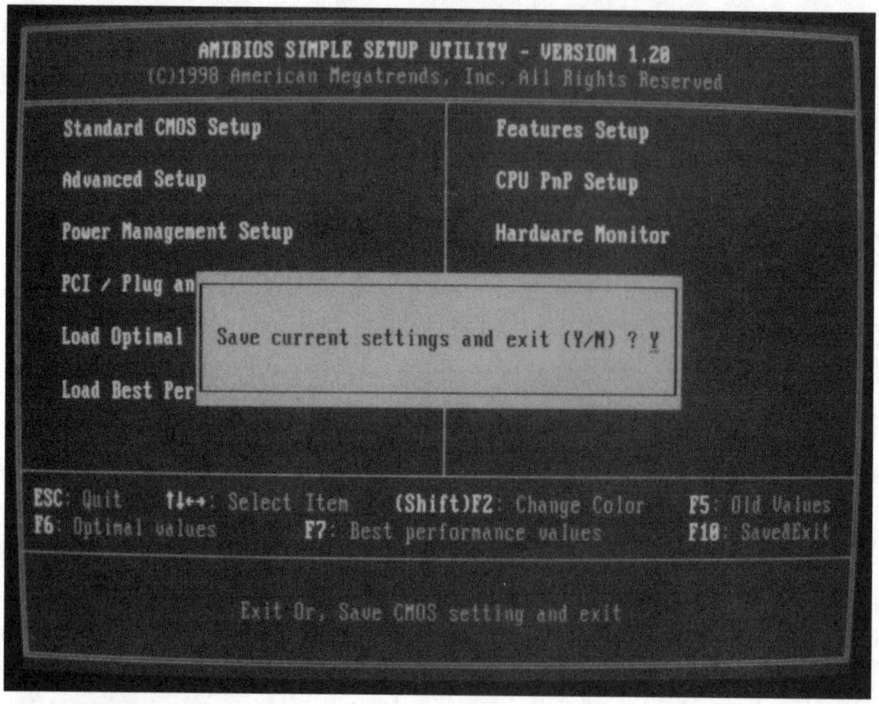

Save and exit.

CHAPTER 5

Building an AMD Athlon in a Midtower Case

Step 1. Case Preparation

The sides of this midtower case, also known as "lids" for the easy access they provide, are each held in place by two screws on the back of the case. Both lids must be removed in order to provide access to both sides of the drive bays. The lids are held from bowing outward by a series of metal tabs that lock into the skeleton of the case. After removing the two screws, slide the lid back about a half an inch, at which point it lifts easily off.

In most instances, the next step in case preparation is installing the I/O shield or punching out openings in a permanent shield and inserting standoffs in the motherboard pan to hold the motherboard. However, when a case, motherboard, CPU, and

Figure 5.1

Removing the lid screw.

RAM are ordered from a single mail-order vendor (the recommended way to buy mail order), all of these components sometimes arrive installed in the case. Rather than faking I/O shield and standoff installation, which is amply illustrated by the other three systems in this book, we decided to take the opportunity to point out that many vendors ship these parts installed to save on packaging and to minimize returns due to assembly problems.

AMD recommends the use of an additional case fan with their Athlon CPU. These inexpensive devices are known as "muffin" fans and increase the airflow through the case. Generally speaking, such fans are labeled on the back of the motor, meaning air is pulled in through the unlabeled side and exhausted through the labeled, or back, side.

Figure 5.2

Back side of muffin fan.

The majority of midtower cases provide a snap-in holder for mounting a muffin fan at the bottom of the front panel. The same assembly often covers or holds the case speaker. Remove the snap-in holder from the case, and mount the fan such that the label on the fan motor will be visible from the inside of the case when installed.

Figure 5.3

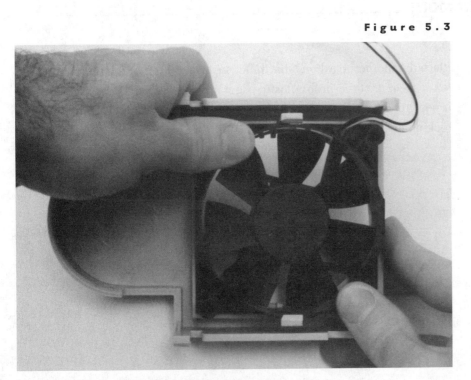

Mounting the muffin fan in the holder.

Finally, snap the completed assembly back into place. The fan is powered by the motherboard, so it won't be connected until a later stage. Once the system is built, you should double-check that the muffin fan is drawing air into the case, since the ATX power supply fan exhausts air from the case, and this will maximize airflow.

Figure 5.4

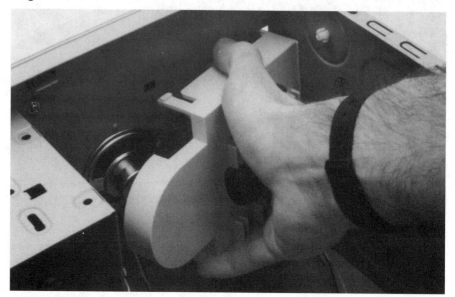

Snapping the assembly into place.

Step 2. Installing Memory

Place the motherboard on a hard, flat surface, on top of the nonconductive foam sheet or static-proof plastic bag it arrived in. This Asus motherboard is equipped with three DIMM slots, the black horizontal objects with white locking levers on either side at the bottom right of Figure 5.5.

Figure 5.5

Asus motherboard.

We are installing two 128-MB PC-100 DIMMs in this system for a total of
256 MB of SDRAM. The white locking levers on both sides of the DIMM
slots must be opened before installing a memory module. The DIMMs are
keyed with two notches on the contact edge so they can only be inserted
into the slot in the proper orientation.

Figure 5.6

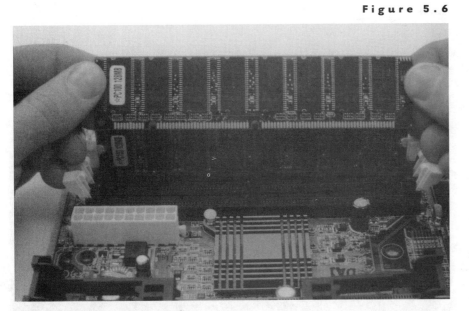

128-MB DIMM over the socket.

Press evenly on both ends of the DIMM with your thumbs until the white locking levers draw up. It can take a reasonable amount of pressure to seat the DIMM, but don't try to dig one corner in first to get it started. Never pull up on the levers to try to encourage the DIMM to seat easier.

Figure 5.7

Seating the DIMM with two thumbs.

Both DIMMs are installed, and the locking levers are full engaged. Always refer to your motherboard manual to see which slots must be filled first when you are installing fewer DIMMs than the number of available DIMM slots.

Figure 5.8

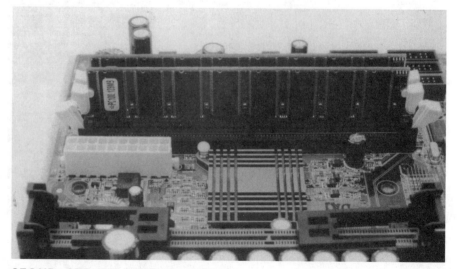

256 MB of PC-100 SDRAM installed.

Step 3. Attaching the Athlon Heat Sink
and Installing on the Motherboard

The Athlon, or AMD K7, is a cartridge-type CPU that generates more heat than any other CPU currently used in PCs. There are a variety of heat sink and fan combinations available to cool the Athlon, some of which sport two fans for increased cooling capacity.

Figure 5.9

Athlon CPU.

The back of the Athlon package contains several holes designed for mounting different types of heat sinks. The dual-fan heat sink locks to the Athlon at four points.

Figure 5.10

Athlon and heat sink mounting provisions.

The heat sink hooks onto the Athlon package at the bottom, then is locked through the two holes at the top by means of a flip-over locking lever. Make sure the heat sink is flat against the Athlon with the hardware properly engaged in the holes before pushing over the locking lever.

Figure 5.11

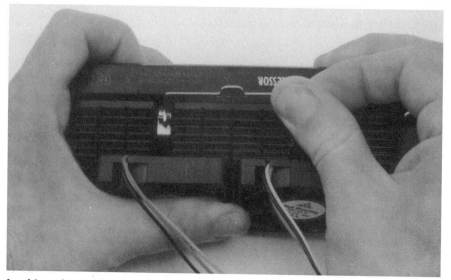

Locking the Athlon to the heat sink.

Always check the motherboard manual for any switches or jumpers that must be set for CPU speed and voltage. The Asus motherboard is capable of autodetecting the Athlon and choosing the right settings, provided the selection switches are set for that default mode. Even if your motherboard arrives with the CPU already installed, it's no guarantee that any switches have been set properly, so check that manual!

Figure 5.12

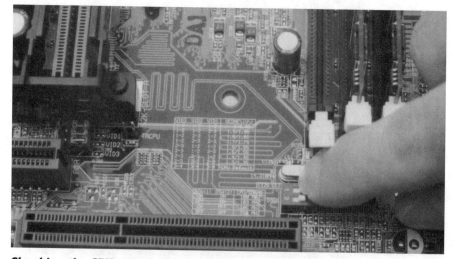

Checking the CPU switch settings.

Raise the Slot A supports that will hold the Athlon and heat sink assembly. Some motherboards also provide hardware for supporting the back end of the heat sink, which must be installed separately.

Line up the notch in the contact edge of the Athlon with the key in the slot. This key prevents the processor from being installed backwards. Then lower the Athlon into the supports.

Figure 5.13

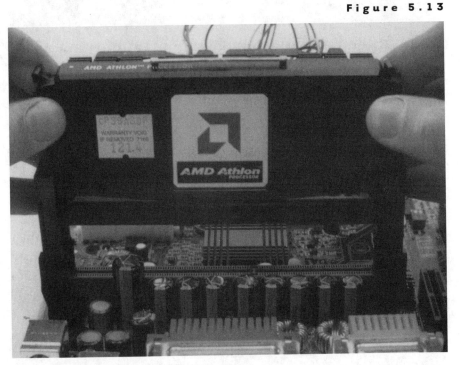

Lowering the Athlon into the Slot A supports.

The tabs on either end of the Athlon package must be pushed in for the Athlon to seat properly. Once the Athlon is lowered into position, push the tabs in, and push down on both ends of the processor to seat it in the slot.

Figure 5.14

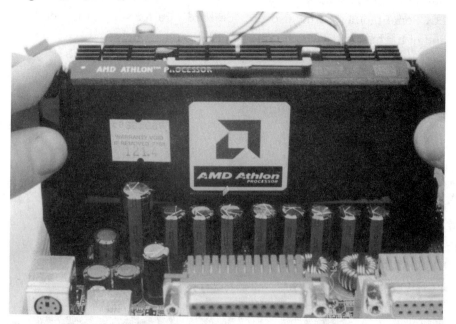

Seating the Athlon with tabs pushed in.

Once the Athlon is properly seated in the socket, the tabs must be pulled out to lock it into place. This should not require much force, and if they don't snap out easily, make sure that the Athlon is seated all the way into the slot.

Figure 5.15

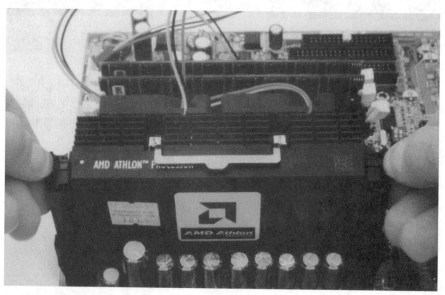

Locking the Athlon into place.

The final step before the motherboard is ready for installation into the case is to connect the heat sink fan. Since this heat sink uses two fans, it requires two connectors. The motherboard power management logic is actually capable of saving energy by controlling these fans and running only one or neither of them when the processor is in a low-power condition.

Figure 5.16

Connecting the heat sink fans.

Step 4. Installing Motherboard and Adapters

As mentioned previously, the mail-order vendor for this system actually shipped it with the motherboard installed, so we didn't need to line up the standoffs or install the I/O core shield. Both of these operations are well illustrated in our Pentium III minitower and Pentium II midtower systems. Nonetheless, it's always good practice to count the standoffs in the motherboard pan (six in this case) and make sure you find that number of holes on the motherboard that line up with these standoffs before you start putting screws in.

Figure 5.17

Screwing in the motherboard.

The next step is to connect the ATX power supply to the motherboard. The power supply should not be plugged into an outlet at this point. The power supply connector contains 20 wires and is keyed so it can only be inserted one way. The connector should be pushed down until the single locking lever on the connector clicks over the projection on the receptacle, locking the connector into place.

Figure 5.18

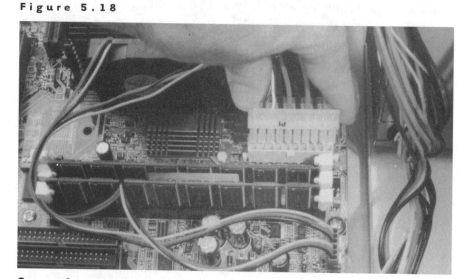

Connecting power to the motherboard.

The first card we will install in the Athlon is a 10/100BaseT network adapter. This PCI adapter, which costs only $10, has no switches or jumpers to set; like most PCI adapters, it is fully Plug and Play.

The adapter card is mounted in the farthest slot for maximum spacing between the installed adapters. This reduces port congestion on the back of the system, making it easier to connect the various cables to these adapters once the build is finished. Always make sure that the connector port on the adapter is fully exposed through the opening on the back of the case before you screw the adapters in.

Figure 5.19

Securing the 10/100BaseT adapter.

This V.90 56-Kb/s modem is also a PCI adapter and is also fully Plug and Play. When handling adapters, you should always be careful not to touch the gold contacts slot with your fingers.

PCI adapters usually seat very easily in the slots. If you have a problem seating a PCI adapter, it's probably due to the motherboard being positioned too close to the back of the case. If you run into this situation, check if the case is bent or if the mounting rail where the screws are inserted can be repositioned or bent to conform with the required geometry. In all instances, check that both modem ports are fully accessible from the back of the case, then secure it with a screw.

Figure 5.20

Securing the modem.

An AGP video adapter with 8 MB of video RAM and a 3D processor was selected for this system. There is only a single AGP port on the motherboard, and this is located as closely as possible to the CPU and SDRAM banks.

Figure 5.21

Installing the AGP video adapter.

The AGP adapter is the most likely candidate to become partially dislodged from the slot as it is screwed in. This occurs because the edge of the AGP slot is further from the back of the case than any of the other adapter slots, creating a long lever. The adapter sometimes pivots on the edge of the slot as the port end of the adapter is screwed down, levering the back edge out of contact with the slot. Keep an eye on the slot to see that the whole length of the connector on the adapter remains seated as you tighten the screw.

Step 5. Installing Drives

In order to install the floppy drive, you must first remove one of the 3.5-inch blanks from the front panel of the case. These can normally be popped out from behind with your fingers, but you may occasionally run into a blank that is locked into place, requiring you to remove the front panel of the case. An illustration of removing the front panel from a mid-tower is given in Chapter 6. The top blank is normally the preferred mounting location when more than one opening is available. Slide the drive into the case in the upside-up orientation.

Figure 5.22

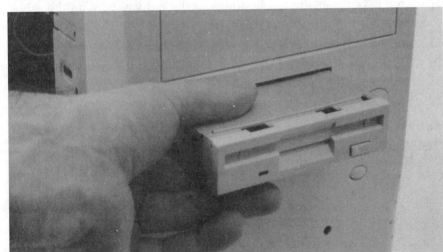

Installing the 1.44-MB floppy drive.

Secure the floppy drive with two screws on each side. It's much easier to install the cables when the drive is held securely. The design of this floppy cage makes it easy to access the back of the installed drive for attaching the ribbon cable, so we didn't preconnect the cable before sliding the drive in.

Figure 5.23

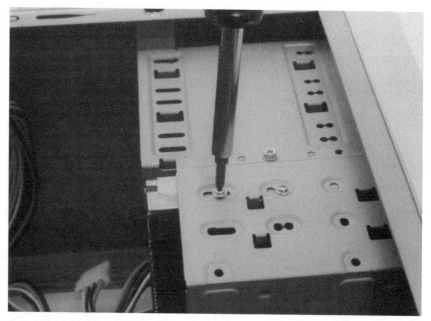

Securing the floppy drive.

Attach the ribbon cable to the floppy with the red key wire on the cable oriented to pin 1 on the floppy drive. Don't assume that keyed cables will only mate one way on floppy drives because this isn't always the case. The pin 1 location is sometimes noted on the backside of the drive rather then next to the connector.

Figure 5.24

Installing the ribbon cable.

The power lead for the floppy drive is one of the small format connectors, only one of which is available on some power supplies. The connector has a shallow indentation on the bottom with a small, angled locking key to help hold it in place. The four-pin connection block on the drive should have a matching plastic tab that fits into the indentation.

Figure 5.25

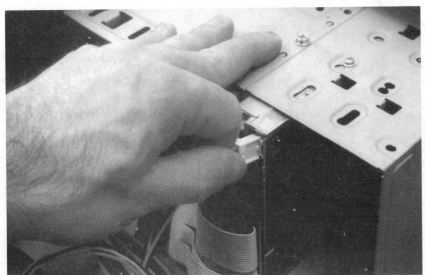

Connecting the floppy drive power.

Now connect the ribbon cable to the motherboard, again following the red-key-wire-on-pin-1 convention. In this case, the cable header is keyed to the motherboard connector with a plugged hole (second from right in lower row on connector).

Figure 5.26

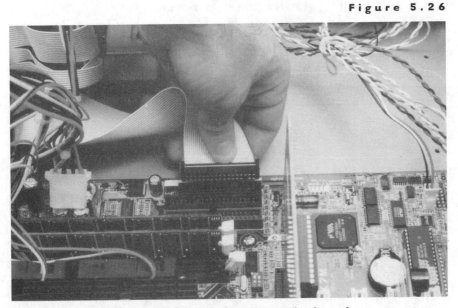

Connecting the floppy ribbon cable to the motherboard.

Next we install our 16-GB UDMA/66 (or Ultra ATA) Maxtor hard drive. We don't need to set any master/slave jumpers in this instance, because the drive is shipped with the default selection of "Single or Master" and we won't be installing a slave on the same cable.

Secure the hard drive in place with two screws from each side.

Figure 5.27

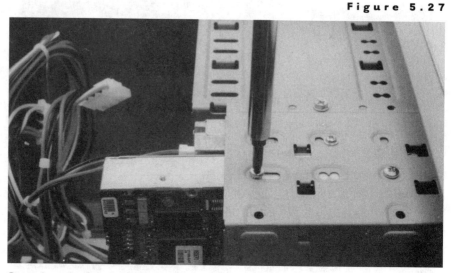

Securing the hard drive.

You can install a non-UDMA/66 as a slave with a UDMA/66 drive, but the master must be at the end of the special 80-conductor cable. This means you can run into trouble getting the cable to reach to a CD-ROM at the top of a midtower for the middle connector, then back again to the motherboard for the other end. The red key wire goes on pin 1, which on hard drives is the end closest to the power connector.

Figure 5.28

Connecting the 80-conductor Ultra ATA ribbon cable.

The power lead is keyed to fit one way only. It should push into the receptacle at least a quarter of an inch, but they never go in all the way to the raised stop on the connector, and it would probably break the drive to pull it out if it did get in that far.

Figure 5.29

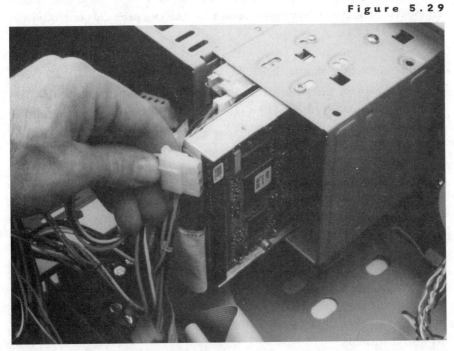

Connecting the hard drive power.

Now connect the far end of the ribbon cable to the primary IDE controller on the motherboard. The slightly more expensive 80-conductor ribbon cables are often keyed for the motherboard, but as always, make sure that the red key wire is oriented at the pin 1 end of the connector. Although there are 80 conductors in the cable, there are only 40 actual connection pins, since the 40 extra conductors are all tied to ground for electrical noise immunity.

Figure 5.30

Connecting the 80-conductor ribbon cable to the primary controller.

We now connect a standard IDE ribbon cable to the secondary IDE controller so we can plan the cable routing for our remaining two drives. Ribbon cable makers often skimp on cable length to save a few pennies or the connectors may be placed too close together to span the distances you need. This cable header is not keyed, so we follow the red-wire-on-pin-1 convention, which is in the same direction as with the cables already installed.

A second hard drive is being added to this system to support a hardware dual-boot option. The Asus motherboard allows you to chose which IDE master you want to boot from in CMOS. This means you can install two hard drives—a primary and secondary master—and install a different operating system on each, Windows and Linux in our case. This saves a lot of aggravation fooling around with software dual-boot loaders and restrictive drive formats.

Figure 5.31

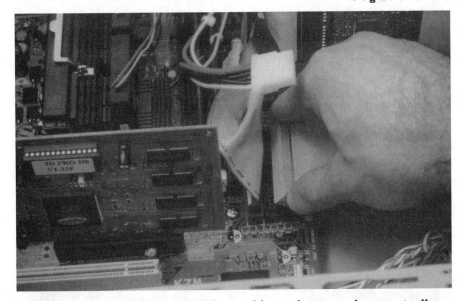

Connecting the standard IDE ribbon cable to the secondary controller.

Although it is good practice to connect the master device to the end of an
IDE ribbon cable, with lower-performance drives it usually doesn't make
any difference. The center connector on the IDE ribbon cable is used here
due to cable length considerations. The red dotted key wire is up toward
the power connector and pin 1. The use of a dotted red key wire rather
then one of solid red is common and sometimes difficult to discern. Set
the selection jumper to "Master" before installing the drive. Setting the
master and slave jumpers is clearly illustrated in the Pentium III build in
Chapter 4.

Figure 5.32

Connecting the IDE cable to the second hard drive.

Many power supplies are equipped with three large-format drive connectors and one small-format connector, and since the connectors are placed on two leads in pairs, drives that are close together must share the same lead. This power supply actually has three leads from the supply with six connectors.

Before installing the CD drive, set the jumper to "Slave" and connect the CD sound cable. Pop out the plastic cover for the top bay in the case, and slide the CD drive in from the front.

Figure 5.33

Installing the CD drive.

Secure the CD drive in place with four fine-thread screws, two from either side. CD drives are not as rigid as hard drives, and the tray that ejects to accept CDs has a long travel, so it's important not to force screws into the drive. If you have trouble getting four screws into the drive easily, try loosening the screws on the other side (retightening them after four screws are in), and if that doesn't work, try a different drive bay.

Connect the secondary ribbon cable to the CD drive, with the red dotted key wire on pin 1. Pin 1 on CD drives is generally toward the power connector, as with hard drives.

Figure 5.34

Connecting the secondary IDE cable.

The drive is shown here with all the connections made, including power at the top and the small CD sound connector at the bottom. If the ribbon cables in your system have a great deal of slack, it's a good idea to loosely tape or tie them together, but I discourage the use of electrical tie-wraps, which are difficult to remove without damaging the cable should the need arise.

Figure 5.35

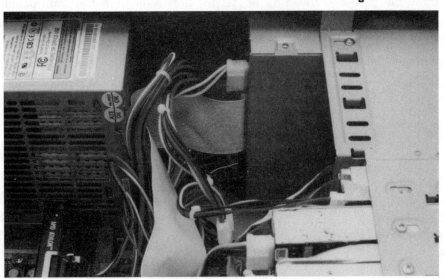

CD drive with all connections made.

Step 6. Motherboard Connections

Connect the muffin fan to the auxiliary fan connection point on the motherboard. When you build a system with one or more case fans, leave the cover or lid off when powering up the system for the first time. Then make sure you confirm that air is being drawn into the case by at least one fan and exhausted by at least one fan.

Figure 5.36

Connecting the case fan.

You usually need to consult the motherboard manual in order to determine the proper connection points for the leads from the front-panel switches, LEDs, and internal speaker. The case speaker and switches will work as long as they are connected to the correct set of pins, but the LEDs will not light if the leads are put on backwards. This doesn't hurt the LEDs; just reverse the position of the connector on the pins if this occurs.

Figure 5..37

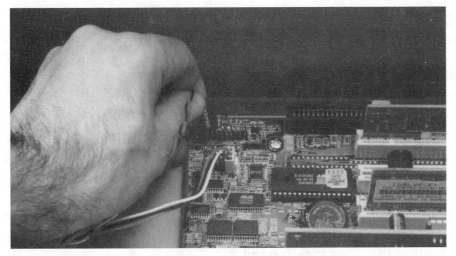

Connecting front-panel leads.

The CD sound connection is made to a special port on the motherboard when the motherboard includes onboard sound capabilities.

Figure 5.38

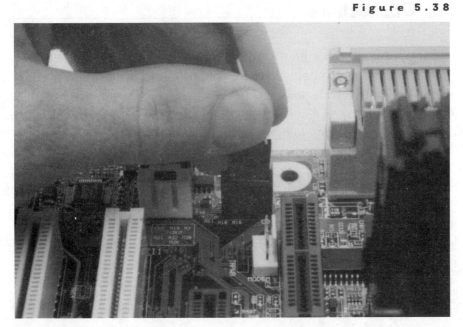

Connecting CD sound (shown outside case for illustration).

The completed system from the back is shown in Figure 5.39. The motherboard I/O core connectors are all located in the ATX opening next to the power supply, while the ports on the adapters installed are visible through the slots in the back of the case. Before moving on to exterior connections, pick up the whole PC, turn the open side down, and gently shake it back and forth while listening for screws rolling about. If you do hear a rolling

Figure 5.39

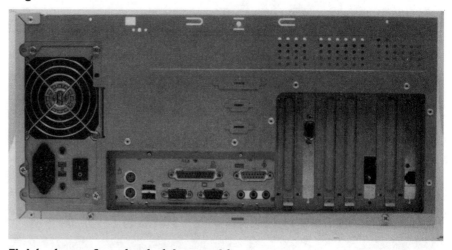

Finished case from back, lying on side.

screw that stops without falling out, you must locate and remove it before powering on the PC.

Step 7. Making Exterior Connections

Before plugging in the power supply, check the voltage switch to make sure it is set to the proper voltage for your country. Also note the position of the external override power switch if your system is equipped with one. The power switch on the front panel of the PC will not turn the computer on unless this override switch is also turned on. It's normal to leave the switch on at all times, unless you are working on the PC and want to leave the cord plugged in as a ground.

Figure 5.40

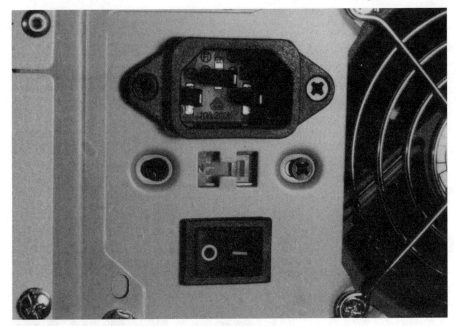

Checking the power supply voltage switch.

The PS/2-style mouse and keyboard are connected to their ports in the I/O core. Mouse and keyboard connectors are molded with a raised plastic ridge or arrow that is oriented in the "up" direction relative to the motherboard. Most mouse and keyboard connectors are also color-coded—purple for the keyboard and green for the mouse.

Figure 5.41

Connecting the PS/2 mouse.

The 15-pin video connector (less than 15 pins are often present) is shaped like a trapezoid and can only be attached one way. Look carefully at the shape and the connector and the port before making the connection, because if you bash away at it in the dark, you may bend one of the pins in the connector.

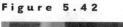

Figure 5.42

Connecting the monitor.

Modems all offer two connection ports. One is labeled "line" and must be cabled to the telephone jack with a standard modular phone cord; the other is labeled "phone," and here you can plug in your phone for normal use. If you are daisy-chaining a number of computer modems, fax machines, and phones, try to connect the computer modems to the wall outlet first.

After powering on the PC and checking the fan airflow directions, power down again, then replace the remaining lid and secure it with two screws. This PC required no CMOS setup entries at all, since the motherboard auto-detected the drives and CPU. However, it's a good idea to enter CMOS setup and familiarize yourself with all the options the motherboard supports. The final step is to install an operating system, as covered in Chapter 8.

Figure 5.43

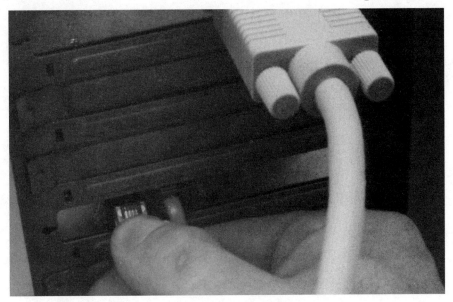

Connecting the phone handset to the modem.

CHAPTER 6

Building a Pentium II or Celeron in a Midtower Case

Step 1. Removing the Cover and Preparing the Case

Minitower and midtower cases are often chosen by do-it-yourselfers, in part because of their lower cost and in part because they are really an easier design to work with. The main advantage of the tower-style design is the option for a removable motherboard pan—make sure the case you buy is so equipped. A standard feature of the ATX case is the large, standard-sized rectangular opening (right side, halfway down) where the motherboard-mounted I/O ports will be exposed for connection.

We begin by removing the four screws that hold the midtower cover to the frame of the case. The easiest way to identify which screws to take out is to note which screw heads are covering some of the painted edge of the cover. Other screws, which you don't want to loosen, hold the power supply or internal framing in place.

Figure 6.1

A standard ATX midtower from the back.

Once the screws are removed, the cover may still be stubborn about sliding free. Use both hands, placing the fingers along the top and side of the cover and using the thumbs to push against the back of the case. If the cover still doesn't want to come free, try lifting a little at the back top edge, which frees the side channels of the cover from the base of the case.

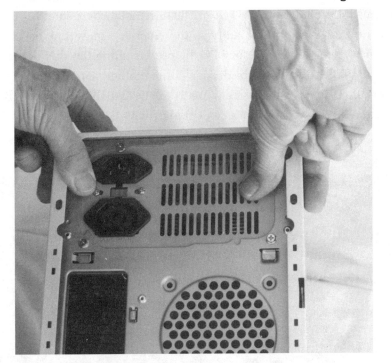

Freeing the cover from the case.

After the cover is off, remove the parts shipped loose in the case, usually a bag of screws, plastic or rubber feet for the case, the speaker assembly, and any other loose parts. Next, remove the motherboard pan, which is usually held in place by two or three screws and depends on an open hinge for structural support. Note carefully how the pan comes out (i.e., flip down and slide right or straight up and slide left), because it will go back in the same way.

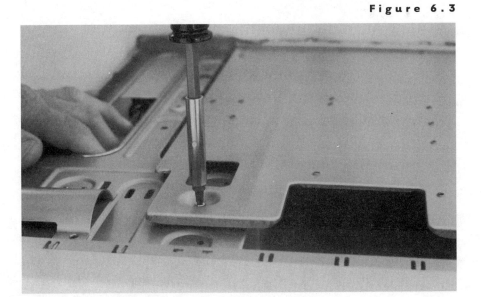

Removing the motherboard pan.

One of the most important steps you want to perform at this point is installing the shield for the I/O core. The thin metal cover shields RF emissions and frames the ports tightly so that dust and bugs (the insect kind) stay out of your warm and cozy PC. Before installing the shield, match it against the I/O ports on the back edge of the motherboard to ensure that it fits and that you get the orientation correct. The shield is actually not much thicker than tinfoil, so it can't stand rough handling.

F i g u r e   6 . 4

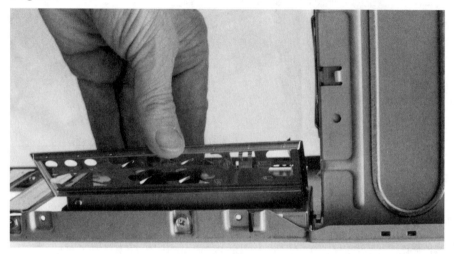

Installing the I/O—shield inside view.

Figure 6.5 shows the I/O shield properly installed in the case. On this shield, you can see the pictograph symbols for the device ports: mouse, keyboard, speakers, and so on. The only thing that holds the shield in place is the spring force of the folded edges, which press against the sides

F i g u r e   6 . 5

Properly installed shield.

of the openings. All of the little tabs will press against the various ports, providing a little structural stiffness and grounding.

The speaker assembly may already be installed when the case is purchased; in other instances, you must snap it into place yourself. Four plastic legs lock into slots in the metal front of the case. The back of the speaker assembly provides support for any full-length adapter cards you might install later. This speaker is used primarily for the beeps and ticks produced by the system during boot time or in case of failure. It doesn't have any connection to the sound card, which requires external speakers.

Step 2. Mounting the Motherboard

The first feature of our Intel AL440LX motherboard that will jump out at anybody who has built a PC in the last 15 years is the lack of a CPU socket. The motherboard utilizes instead a CPU slot, Slot 1 in this instance, positioned horizontally just behind the edge-mounted I/O ports at the top right of Figure 6.6. The adapter card bus slots, thin black or white rectangles oriented vertically in our picture, are as follows: one AGP connector (right behind the round battery), two 16-bit ISA slots, four 32-bit PCI slot.

Figure 6.6

Intel AL440LX motherboard.

The ATX design provides for all of the standard I/O ports to be mounted directly on the edge of the motherboard. There are five or six standard "cores" defined by Intel for arranging the port connectors. From left to right in Figure 6.7: the stacked PS/2-style keyboard and mouse ports, the stacked USB ports, parallel printer and game port along the top, two serial ports and sound connectors along the bottom.

Figure 6.7

ATX motherboard I/O core.

The three black horizontal slots in Figure 6.8 are for DIMMs (dual inline memory modules) that replace the older 72-pin SIMMs. The white latching mechanisms on either end must be opened prior to installing the DIMMs and are automatically engaged as

Figure 6.8

DIMM slots and drive connectors.

the module is properly seated. The white connector block below the DIMM slots to the right is the 20-pin female power supply connector, arranged in two rows of 10. To the left of the power supply connector are two 40-pin male connectors, the primary and secondary IDE (Integrated Device Electronics) ports. The 34-pin male floppy connector is below the power supply connector.

The black framework rising up from the motherboard is held in position around the CPU slot (Slot 1) by four captured screws. The retention mechanism retains the Pentium II SEC (single-edged cartridge) and heat sink. The Celeron and heat sink require a top lockdown piece for the retention mechanism.

Figure 6.9

Slot 1 retention mechanism installation.

The ATX motherboard is mounted to the pan using brass standoffs only! The holes intended for mounting screws are each surrounded by a shiny ring of solder. No more irritating plastic sliding mounts. The holes in the pan are labeled for different motherboard forms, but the best approach is still to line up the holes by eye and add standoffs wherever possible. The standoffs can be tightened with a nutdriver, a small socket, or pliers. Always count the number of standoffs you use and make sure you put in the same number of screws. Otherwise, you have misplaced a standoff that is waiting to short-circuit your motherboard when the system is plugged in.

Figure 6.10

Securing the motherboard with screws.

Step 3. Installing the CPU and Heat Sink

Both the Pentium II and Celeron CPUs are packaged as SECs, but the Celeron lacks the L2 cache and locking package of the Pentium II. Both SECs are designed to accept *active heat sinks*, a heat sink cooled by a fan. The Pentium II is equipped with a one-piece active heat sink for which the Pentium II cartridge provides the locking receptacles. The Celeron requires a two-piece assembly: the active heat sink and a backing piece to provide the locking.

Figure 6.11

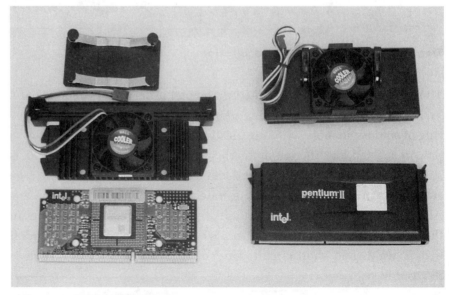

Celeron and Pentium II with active heat sinks.

The Pentium II heat sink is locked in place with two levers on either side of the fan. The levers engage four metal clamps, which enter the standard openings in the back of the Pentium II cartridge.

Figure 6.12

Locking the heat sink lever.

The Celeron SEC comes without mounting provisions for a heat sink, but it does have four holes drilled in the circuit board. A spring-loaded backing plate with four male hold-downs is mounted on the back of the SEC, where you can see all the solder points for the CPU legs coming through in a square.

Figure 6.13

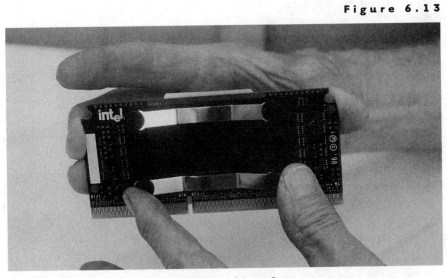

Positioning the Celeron heat sink backing plate.

The actual heat sink is then pressed over the CPU side of the SEC and locked into place by the four hold-downs protruding through the card from the backing plate. You must apply even pressure during this operation, because it takes a reasonable amount of force to compress the backing plate springs enough to lock on. Make sure that you get the orientation right the first time, because the heat sink is very difficult to remove once installed.

Figure 6.14

Positioning the Celeron heat sink.

The Celeron processor, unlike the Pentium II, is not automatically locked into place by the retention mechanism when mounted in the Slot 1 connector. An extra plastic cover piece fits over the retention mechanism to lock the Celeron in place.

Figure 6.15

Celeron mounted—top view.

Both Pentium II and Celeron heat sink fans use a dedicated connector on the ATX motherboard for power. The ATX Intel motherboard provides three different power points for add-on fans. The proper connector to use with the CPU heat sink is located between the DIMM banks and the Slot 1 connector. This allows the motherboard power management to shut down the fan when the CPU is off and the system is in a suspended state.

Figure 6.16

Pentium II fan connected to the motherboard.

Finally, you can see the Pentium II mounted on the motherboard, which in turn is mounted on the removable pan. The Pentium II is locked into place by the retention mechanism alone, without the top piece required by the Celeron.

Figure 6.17

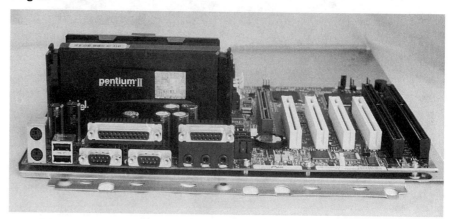

Pentium II and motherboard on the pan.

Step 4. Installing RAM

We install the DIMMs with the motherboard and pan still outside the case. In Figure 6.18, you can clearly see the alignment notches in the contact edge of the DIMM, which are matched to the two blocking keys in the DIMM socket, making it impossible to fully insert the DIMM in the wrong orientation. Lower the white thumb tabs on either side of the DIMM socket before inserting the module.

Figure 6.18

Seating the second DIMM.

The new-style DIMM sockets have one disadvantage over the older style "lean-in" SIMM sockets. You may need to apply a good deal of force to make the DIMM engage the locking mechanism and seat properly. Definitely a two-thumb job.

Figure 6.19

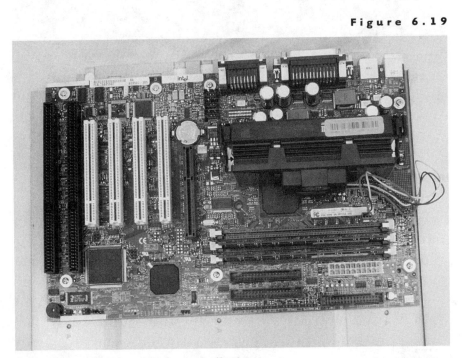

ATX motherboard ready for installation.

In Figure 6.19, we can see the ATX motherboard mounted on the pan, with the Pentium II heat sink installed and the fan connected to the "fan 3" power point. The two 32-MB DIMMs of SDRAM are installed.

Step 5. Installing the Motherboard Pan and Making Case Connections

When installing the motherboard pan back into the case, you want to be very careful that you don't crush any cables or onboard components while moving the pan into place. Normally, the pan hinges along one edge when positioned properly. As soon as the pan is properly positioned, waste no time reattaching the screws that hold the pan to the frame.

Figure 6.20

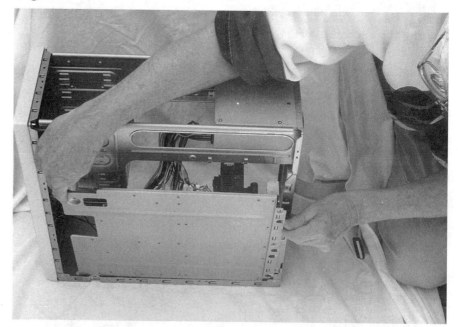

Installing the motherboard pan.

Figure 6.21

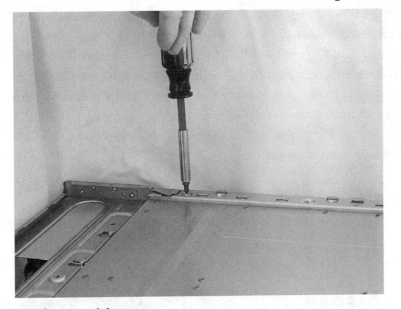

Securing the pan with screws.

The 20-pin power lead from the ATX power supply replaces the P8 and P9 connectors used for almost 15 years in AT-style systems. The connector is keyed to go in one way only, and it is located in an easily accessed spot. Make sure the power supply is not plugged into the wall yet! The power supply should not be plugged in until you have finished making all of your connections and screwed in all of the adapters you are installing in your PC.

Figure 6.22

Connecting the ATX power supply lead.

The ATX design places all of the attachment points for the case LEDs (lights) and switches along the front edge of the motherboard. LED and switch leads are usually labeled—"power," "HDD" "(hard drive access)," "key lock," and so forth—with little stickers right on the leads. If the leads aren't labeled, you'll have to follow them back to the front panel of the case and read the faceplate to identify them. Note that the power switch lead is a logic switch; it doesn't actually connect or disconnect 115 VAC like a light switch. The action of the switch can be controlled in CMOS setup once the system is assembled.

Figure 6.23

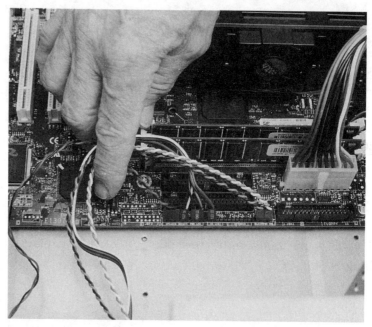

Case leads for the LEDs, case speaker, and switches.

With the motherboard pan installed in the ATX case, you can now see the I/O core ports through the openings in the metal I/O shield. Motherboard manufacturers provide a standard metal bezel that fits around their particular arrangement of ports, often including pictorial or text labels for the port functions.

Figure 6.24

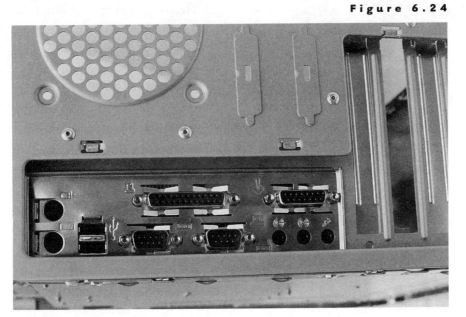

I/O core from the back.

Step 6. Installing the Drives

In most cases, both tower and desktop, the 3.5-inch drives are mounted in a removable "cage." This design allows for large motherboards to extend out into the space beside the cage, where they would block access to the drives if the cage were not removable. If your case allows open access to both sides of the cage, and you are comfortable working with your hands in a cramped area, you can skip removing the cage. However, the majority of the time the job goes easier with the cage out, despite the extra steps. Examine how the facade is held to the front of the case. This is normally accomplished with either screws or by six clusters of spring fingers, as in our case. Pry the facade away from the case, starting at a corner and working your way around.

With the facade removed, you can see that the case manufacturer always assumes that at least one CD-ROM (5.25-inch drive) and one floppy (3.5-inch) drive will be installed in every case, because the openings in the sheet metal would otherwise be potential avenues for RF interference.

Figure 6.25

Front of midtower with the faceplate removed.

The first step in installing the drives is to remove the drive cage from the case. The typical drive cage is attached with a couple of screws and a spring steel release on the bottom. Handling the drives and screwing them in is much easier with the cage out, even when access in the case appears good. The frustration you'll save on the first dropped screw or bent pin is well worth the extra work.

Figure 6.26

Removing the drive cage.

When building a PC with an IDE hard drive, you'll almost always want to set the select jumper on the drive to "master." The exception is if you will install your CD drive as the master on the secondary connector, sometimes necessitated by cable length or other considerations, in which case you should select "single" on the hard drive, if it's an option. Set the jumper before you secure the drive in the cage; it's easier. In our single-hard-drive, single-CD-drive system, the hard drive will be the "master" and the CD drive will be the "slave," both attached to the same ribbon cable.

Figure 6.27

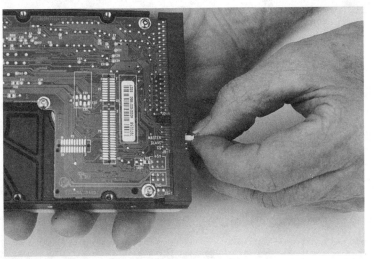

Installing the "Master" jumper on hard drive.

The hard drive is secured with four screws, usually the coarse-thread type, and the end of the drive with the connectors must point toward the inside of the case. There are usually a couple rows of holes in the cage; make sure the holes that you pick will allow the screw heads to clear the case opening when you put the cage back in.

Figure 6.28

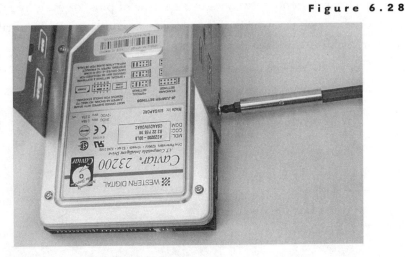

Securing the hard drive in the cage.

Install the 3.5-inch floppy drive, using four fine-thread screws to attach it to the cage. The drive must be mounted with the screws as far forward in the slots as possible. Otherwise, the faceplate of the floppy won't line up with the front facade of the case.

Figure 6.29

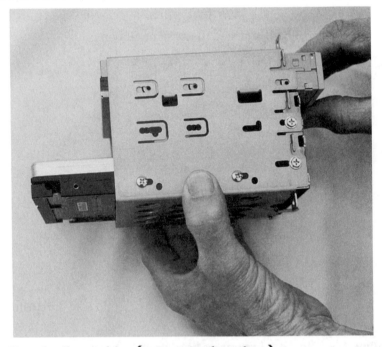

Installing the floppy drive (note screw locations).

Always install the ribbon cable on the floppy drive before returning the cage to the case. One of the most common mistakes made by beginning and experienced PC assemblers alike is misaligning the floppy drive ribbon connector. This can be caused by failing to make the connection with the red key wire to the pin 1 or 2 side of the connector, by accidentally forcing the connector end between a vertical row of pins, or even by missing an entire horizontal row. All of these mistakes can normally be attributed to poor visibility once the drive is installed in the case.

Figure 6.30

Installing the ribbon cable with the drive out.

As the cage is being installed back into the case, you can see that the ribbon cable is already connected to the floppy drive and has been fed through the opening prior to sliding the cage in. Note also the positions of the screws securing the floppy drive in the case, all the way forward in their slots, which is the norm. The hard drive is mounted in the second row of screw holes from the bottom, as these correspond with the extra cutouts in the front of the case.

Figure 6.31

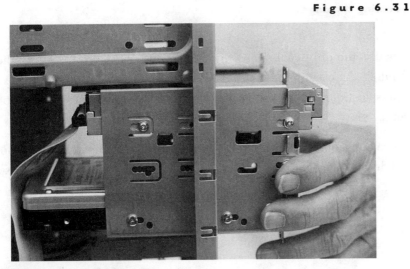

Installing the drive cage.

Don't forget to reinstall the screws that hold the cage in the frame, even though it snaps into place. In Figure 6.32, the CD drive has already been installed in the top bay, even though you may find it easier to align if you wait until you restore the plastic facade to the case front. The faceplate of the CD drive should be flush with the faceplate of the floppy drive.

Figure 6.32

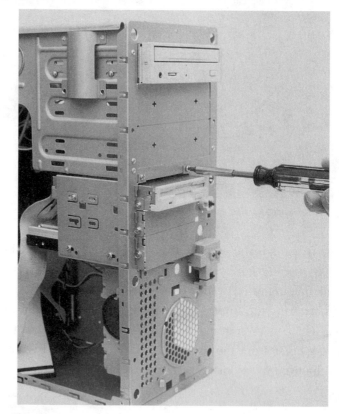

Securing the cage.

Usually, the only cable you can actually attach before installing the CD drive in the case is the patch cable for sound (the connector to the left). The selection jumper, between the sound cable and the ribbon cable, is set to "slave."

Since our motherboard has built-in sound, the audio patch cable from the CD drive attaches directly to the motherboard. If your system has a sound card, the audio patch cable will be attached to it.

Figure 6.33

Connecting the CD sound cable to the motherboard.

The floppy ribbon cable is connected to the controller with the red key wire to pin 1. This cable header was keyed with a plugged hole, as shown in Figure 6.34. See our Athlon build in Chapter 5 for more drive connection details.

Figure 6.34

Floppy cable installation (for illustration only).

Both ribbon cables have been installed on the motherboard, with the red key wire in the ribbon toward pin 1 on the connector. The free end of the IDE ribbon cable has been installed on the connector marked "primary." The identical connector marked "secondary" will be used only if you install additional IDE devices in your PC.

Figure 6.35

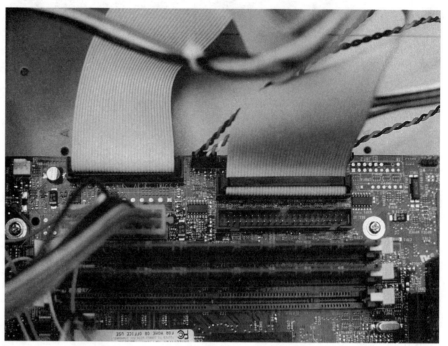

Ribbon cables installed on the motherboard.

Step 7. Installing Adapters

The 56-Kb/s modem in this system is both V.90 and K56flex (Rockwell/Lucent) compatible, which is the standard required by the local Internet service provider where this PC will be installed. The transfer rate of even this fast modem is easily handled by one of our two old-style ISA bus slots.

Don't wait until you are about to put the cover on the case before screwing in adapter cards. Also, examine how the card sits in the bus slot both before and after you put in the single screw. Tightening the screw sometimes causes the adapter to pivot in the bus slot, lifting the contacts on the back section of the adapter away from the fingers in the slot connector. Symptoms of this can be the system's failing to see the adapter as being installed, or failing to boot altogether.

Figure 6.36

Screwing in the modem.

Our Intel motherboard comes with one special slot for use with an AGP (Advanced Graphics Port) video adapter—and nothing else. Like the Pentium II and Celeron SECs, the AGP connector uses two levels of contacts for more control lines on the bus. Thanks to sophisticated bus cycle usage (pipelining and two transfers per cycle) and a basic clock rate double the PCI bus, the AGP can achieve peak speeds four times as fast as a similar PCI adapter.

The AGP slot is located as close to the CPU as possible, since the transfer rates are so fast that the distance the electrical signals must travel becomes a factor. Screw in the adapter as soon as it is seated. The AGP adapter is the most likely candidate to pop out of the bus slot when you put the screw in. The relatively long distance to the back of the case can cause the adapter to pivot on the front edge of the slot, making the far end of the adapter lose contact with the bus.

Figure 6.37

Screwing in the AGP adapter.

Looking at the adapter ports as they appear from the back of the case, the modem ports appear at the bottom and AGP ports at the top. The AGP adapter provides not only the standard SVGA port for connecting your monitor, but also an NTSC (National Television Standards Committee) connector and an S-Video port. The RJ-11 modem ports are for line (to the wall plate), phone (to a phone handset), and speaker and mike for dedicated hands-free operation. The configuration switches for manually setting modem resources can be accessed without opening the case.

Figure 6.38

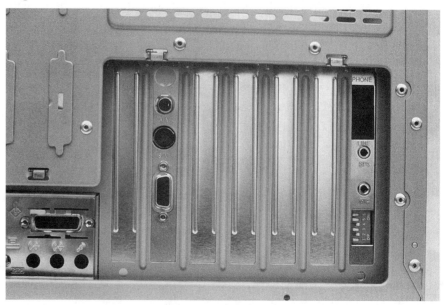

Installed adapters from outside the case.

Step 8. Setting the Motherboard Configuration Jumper and Booting

All of the internal components of the PC have been installed by this point. Pick up the system and shake it gently from side to side, listening for any stray screws rolling around the case. If you hear anything suspicious, don't connect the power cord until you can determine what it is.

Figure 6.39

Top view of the case with everything installed.

Our Intel AL440LX motherboard features software configuration of processor type and speed. Before the system is powered up for the first time, the configuration jumper is set to "maintenance mode." Skip ahead a moment to Step 9 and connect the power cord, keyboard, and monitor, which are needed to continue with the configuration.

Figure 6.40

Motherboard configuration jumper.

When we boot (power on) the system with the Pentium II processor and the configuration jumper set to "maintenance," the system starts at the safe speed of 133 MHz. We choose the Maintenance menu and the processor is correctly identified as a 233-MHz Pentium II (see Figure 6.42), so we exit and choose Save.

Figure 6.41

```
                        BIOS Setup Utility
 Maintenance    Main    Advanced    Security    Power    Boot    Exit

                                               ┌─────────────────────┐
                                               │  Item Specific Help │
    Processor Type        Pentium® II          │                     │
    Processor Speed       133 MHz              │                     │
    Cache RAM             512 KB               │  <Tab>, <Shift-Tab>, or │
    Total Memory          64 MB                │  <Enter> selects field. │
    BIOS Version          4A4LL0X0.86A.0012.P02│                     │
                                               │                     │
    Language:             [English  (US)]      │                     │
    System Time:          [16:52:32]           │                     │
    System Date:          [07/31/1998]         │                     │
                                               │                     │
  ▶ Floppy Options                             │                     │
                                               │                     │
  ▶ Primary IDE Master    [WDC AC23200L]       │                     │
  ▶ Primary IDE Slave     [FX320S]             │                     │
  ▶ Secondary IDE Master  [None]               │                     │
  ▶ Secondary IDE Slave   [None]               │                     │
                                               │                     │

 F1  Help    ↑↓ Select Item    -/+  Change Values      F9  Setup Defaults
 Esc Exit    ↔  Select Menu    Enter Select ▶ Sub-Menu F10 Save and Exit
```

Pentium II main screen.

Figure 6.42

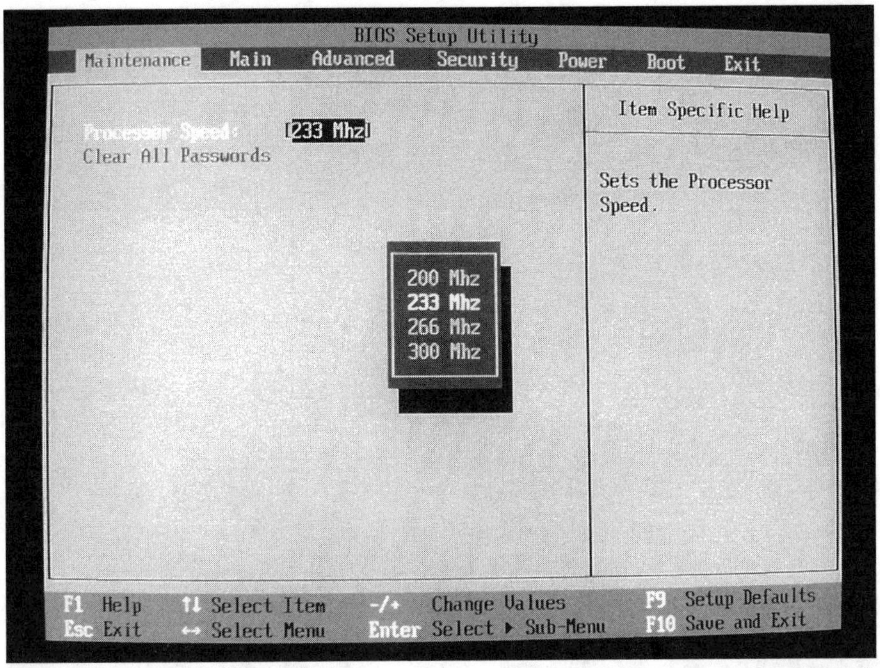

```
                    BIOS Setup Utility
 Maintenance    Main   Advanced   Security   Power   Boot   Exit
                                              ┌─────────────────────┐
                                              │  Item Specific Help │
 Processor Speed:    [233 Mhz]                │                     │
 Clear All Passwords                          │                     │
                                              │ Sets the Processor  │
                                              │ Speed.              │
                         ┌──────────┐         │                     │
                         │ 200 Mhz  │         │                     │
                         │ 233 Mhz  │         │                     │
                         │ 266 Mhz  │         │                     │
                         │ 300 Mhz  │         │                     │
                         └──────────┘         │                     │
                                              │                     │
                                              │                     │
 F1  Help    ↑↓ Select Item   -/+  Change Values    F9  Setup Defaults
 Esc Exit    ↔  Select Menu   Enter Select ▶ Sub-Menu  F10 Save and Exit
```

Pentium II speed setting.

When we boot the system with the Celeron processor installed, the system identifies it as a "Pentium PRO," as shown in Figure 6.43, reflecting the CPU core from which the Celeron was developed. On entering the maintenance menu, the speed is reported correctly at 266 MHz (see Figure 6.44), so exit and choose Save.

Figure 6.43

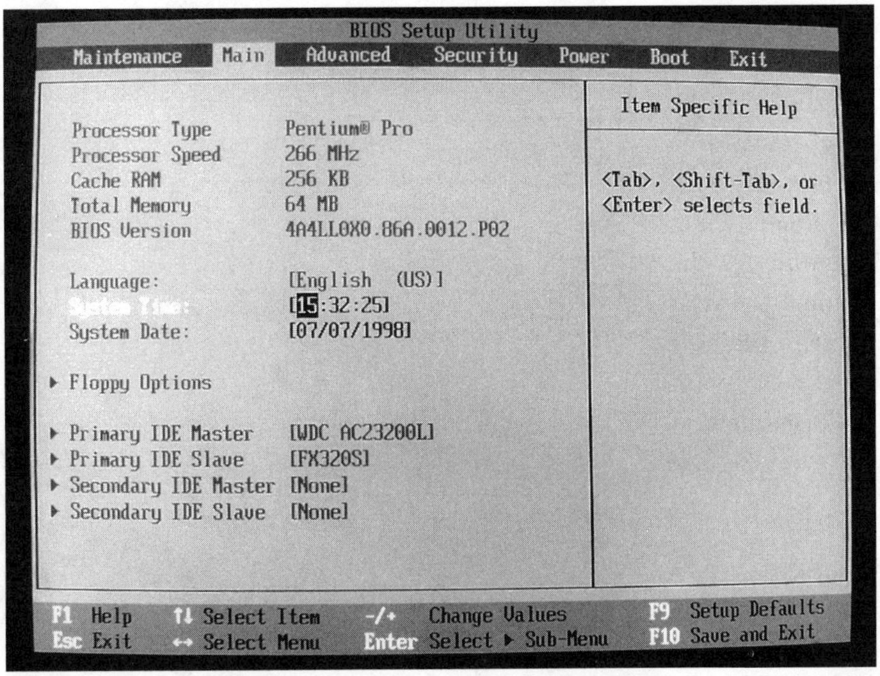

```
                    BIOS Setup Utility
 Maintenance    Main   Advanced   Security   Power   Boot   Exit
                                              ┌─────────────────────┐
                                              │  Item Specific Help │
 Processor Type      Pentium® Pro             │                     │
 Processor Speed     266 MHz                  │                     │
 Cache RAM           256 KB                   │ <Tab>, <Shift-Tab>, or│
 Total Memory        64 MB                    │ <Enter> selects field.│
 BIOS Version        4A4LL0X0.86A.0012.P02    │                     │
                                              │                     │
 Language:           [English  (US)]          │                     │
 System Time:        [15:32:25]               │                     │
 System Date:        [07/07/1998]             │                     │
                                              │                     │
 ▶ Floppy Options                             │                     │
                                              │                     │
 ▶ Primary IDE Master   [WDC AC23200L]        │                     │
 ▶ Primary IDE Slave    [FX320S]              │                     │
 ▶ Secondary IDE Master [None]                │                     │
 ▶ Secondary IDE Slave  [None]                │                     │
                                              │                     │
 F1  Help    ↑↓ Select Item   -/+  Change Values    F9  Setup Defaults
 Esc Exit    ↔  Select Menu   Enter Select ▶ Sub-Menu  F10 Save and Exit
```

Celeron main screen.

Figure 6.44

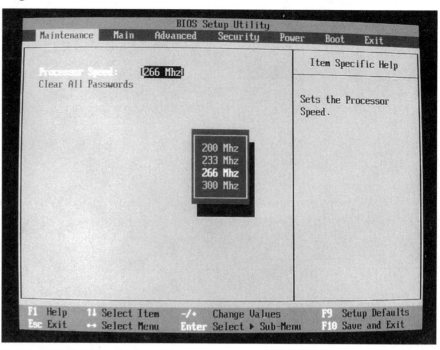

Celeron speed setting.

Make sure you power down the system and set the configuration jumper to "normal" before closing up the case!

Step 9. Closing the Case and Connecting Peripherals

Putting the cover back onto any tower-style case is a little trickier than taking it off, because the large number of locking channels along five edges of the cover must line up properly with the frame. First, examine the channels on your cover to see how they mesh with the case frame.

Figure 6.45

Cover channels.

Next, put the cover on so that the channels in the two bottom edges are all past the back of the case and can slide forward. This normally means the cover should overhang the case by about 2 or 3 inches.

Figure 6.46

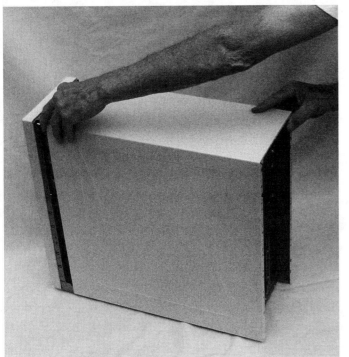

Cover positioned to slide forward.

Slide the cover all the way forward, making sure that the channels along the front edge engage. Any problems encountered during this operation can be solved by a little patient observation to determine where the obstruction is, followed by a little friendly persuasion. Once the cover is on, with all surfaces flush, replace the four screws removed in Step 1.

The system is now ready to be connected to the outside world. The connections for the power supply, modem, monitor, and so forth are nearly identical for all of the systems assembled in this book. The K6 system in Chapter 7 has the best spacing for demonstrating these connections and is heavily illustrated. The first connections to make are the mouse and keyboard. The PS/2 connector used by each has an arrow that points in toward the connector, which may seem silly. However, the arrow is positioned so that it is always at the top of the connector, whereas on the motherboard is at the bottom.

Figure 6.47

Inserting keyboard connector.

Next, we show how to connect a printer cable. The mouse has been plugged in next to the keyboard, and the monitor has been connected to the video adapter at the bottom of Figure 6.48.

Figure 6.48

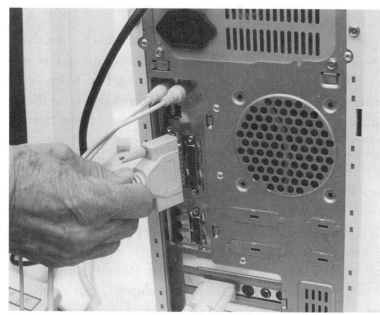

Connecting a printer cable.

The modem phone cord is connected from "line" to the wall, and you can plug your telephone handset into the phone port. External speakers are connected to the speaker port via a standard stereo jack. For detailed photographs of more peripheral connections, see Step 8 in Chapter 7. Otherwise, proceed to Chapter 8 for operating system installation.

Building an AMD K6 Series Socket 7 System in a Desktop Case

Step 1. Removing the Cover and Preparing the Case

The first step in any PC assembly job is removing the cover from the case. Desktop covers are usually attached with five screws in the back, one in each corner and one in the center of the top edge. The screws hold long tabs formed by folding over the sides of the case. You can easily identify which screws are holding the cover on because the screw head will be covering some of the painted metal of the tab.

Figure 7.1

Removing a screw from back of case.

The desktop cover slides back a little, then lifts off. The bottom edges of the cover have channels on the inside that lock onto the edges of the base of the case, so it can take a little pulling to free up the cover. If it's stubborn about sliding back, try lifting the top edge of the back first to reduce the friction between the channels and the frame, then pull back.

Unlike a tower-style case, which is a fairly sound structure even with the cover off, the desktop design requires some extra framing. The cross member running from the back of the case to the 5^1/$_4$-inch in drive cage is held in place by an open hinge and screw. Remove the screw and lift the cross member out for better access while assembling the PC. Other desktop cases may use permanent struts in the top corners for the same purpose.

Figure 7.2

Removing cross member.

Another difference between the desktop and tower-style cases is the lack of a removable motherboard pan in the desktop. The motherboard will be mounted directly on brass standoffs, which are screwed into the holes in the floor of the case. The case speaker in this desktop comes installed. Remove the bag of hardware and any loose parts in the case.

Figure 7.3

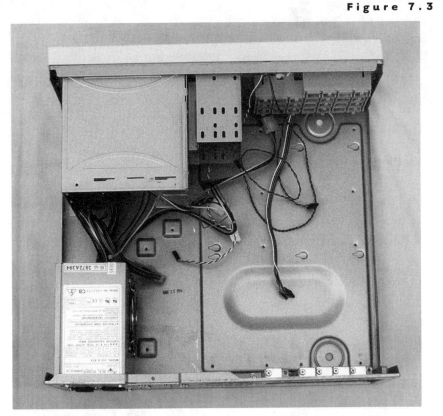

Open desktop case.

An I/O shield matching the motherboard must be installed in the standard opening provided by the ATX standard. Line up the shield against your motherboard first to make sure you get it oriented in the right direction. It's impossible to put the shield in properly once the motherboard is installed. The I/O core on this inexpensive motherboard is relatively simple because of the limited number of onboard options. The only ports included on the motherboard are the PS/2-style keyboard and mouse, the printer ports, and two COM ports.

Figure 7.4

Installing the I/O shield.

Now is as good a time as any to install the feet on the underside of the case. The two main variations on case feet include the plastic snap-in type or the rubber stick-on type that we have in Figure 7.5. The feet protect the surface that the computer stands on from scratches and long-term heat damage or discoloration.

Figure 7.5

Installing rubber feet.

Step 2. Installing the CPU and Heat Sink

Take a good look at the bottom of the CPU and note the one different corner, then lift up the lever to unlock the socket. Line up the keyed corner of the CPU next to the keyed corner of the socket, then flip your hand over so that the CPU seats properly.

Figure 7.6

CPU next to the socket.

Make sure that the CPU sits all the way down, flush with the surface of the socket so that none of the legs are visible. Pull the locking lever back parallel with the motherboard, and nudge it in toward the socket into its home position.

Figure 7.7

Locking the CPU into place.

The Socket 7–style heat sink is somewhat less elegant than the Pentium II and Celeron designs. The basic principle is the same. The metal heat sink structure conducts heat away from the CPU and distributes it onto a large finned area, where the fan provides active cooling.

Figure 7.8

Socket 7 heat sink.

The heat sink is locked in place by a spring steel retainer that connects directly to the socket, with the CPU sandwiched in between. Hook the short end of the locking strip over the mounting point on the socket, then center the heat sink on the CPU.

Figure 7.9

Hooking the short end of the heat sink retainer.

Finally, push the springy end on the locking mechanism down and in to catch the mounting point on the opposite side of the socket.

Figure 7.10

Locking on the heat sink.

The CPU type and speed must be set at this point. Most Socket 7 motherboards accomplish this through a switch block or jumpers. Our Freetech motherboard uses a six-switch block to set the CPU type, speed, and the bus speed. The CPU voltage is autodetected by this particular motherboard. There is no generic guide for setting switches or jumpers; you must follow the specific instructions in your motherboard manual for the CPU you are using.

Figure 7.11

Setting the CPU switch.

Step 3. Installing Memory

We chose to install two 32-MB SDRAM DIMMs in our K6 system, which uses both DIMM sockets on this motherboard. You must open the white thumb latches on either side of the DIMM socket before inserting the module.

The DIMM is keyed by two notches in the connection edge, so it cannot be installed backward. The four shorter white slots in the foreground are for the older-style SIMM memory.

When the DIMM is properly aligned in the slot, it should be seated by gentle, even pressure on both ends of the DIMM. If it doesn't want to seat easily, double-check that the keys are aligned properly, then try applying more pressure with a thumb on both ends of the DIMM.

Figure 7.12

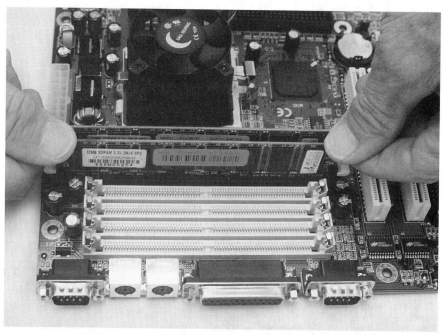

Seating DIMM with two thumbs.

Step 4. Installing the Motherboard

The CPU and heat sink are mounted, and the memory has been installed with the motherboard outside of the case. The next step is to install the motherboard into the case.

Figure 7.13

Motherboard prepared for mounting.

Line up the motherboard in the case so that the I/O core is aligned to mate with the I/O shield, and take note of which screw holes in the floor of the case are lining up with holes in the motherboard. The holes in the motherboard that are intended for mounting are surrounded by a shiny ring of solder. Add enough brass standoffs to the case floor to match all of the possible mounting holes in the motherboard. Count the number of standoffs you use.

Figure 7.14

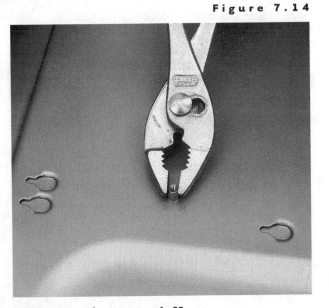

Tightening a brass standoff.

Place the motherboard on top of the standoffs as closely as you can to being correctly aligned. If it isn't quite perfect, pick up the board a fraction of an inch by holding onto a bus slot, and nudge it into place. You don't want to slide the motherboard, since the standoffs may scratch the bottom.

Figure 7.15

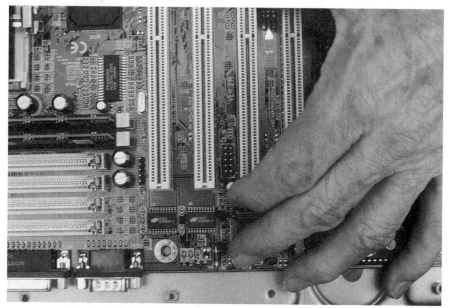

Positioning the motherboard.

When the motherboard is in place, put a screw in the standoff in the center of the back edge to hold it against the I/O shield and still allow a little pivoting if necessary. Put in the rest of the screws, making sure you use the same number of screws as standoffs. If you come out short, you have a standoff in the wrong place waiting to ruin your motherboard, so take it out and start over.

The ATX motherboard is powered by a single 20-pin connector from the power supply. Make sure the power supply is not plugged into the wall before you connect the motherboard, and don't plug the power supply in until you have completely assembled the PC. The connector is keyed to go on one way only.

Figure 7.16

Connecting the power supply.

When you purchase your Socket 7 heat sink and fan, hopefully, units with
an ATX power connector will have become widely available. If your heat
sink unit does have an ATX power connector, it can be hooked directly to
the motherboard, as was the case with Pentium II and Celeron heat sinks.
However, at publication time, the majority of Socket 7 active heat sinks

Figure 7.17

Connecting the heat sink fan.

were being sold with the older AT-style connector, which is a simple inline scheme that attaches to any of the drive leads from the power supply. The disadvantage of this method is that you lose the ability to do power management on the heat sink fan, shutting it down when the CPU is off.

The standard switch and LED leads can be connected at this point. These include power (often blue and white), reset, key lock (optional), hard drive LED (HDD), and speaker. The connectors are labeled on the motherboard and usually on the leads. If the leads aren't labeled, you can follow them back to the front of the case to see where they connect. The speaker connection is for the case speaker, which gives beeps and ticks for status and diagnostics only. The power switch is a "logic" or "software" switch. Settings you can choose later in CMOS setup will determine if the switch immediately shuts the system off and on or if it invokes a standby mode for low power consumption.

Figure 7.18

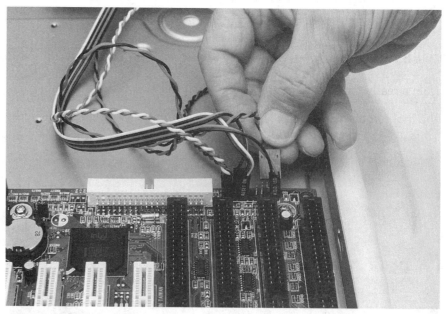

Connecting the speaker lead.

Step 5. Installing Drives

To install drives properly in a desktop case, you must remove the front facade of the case and take out the drive cage. Examine the facade from behind (inside the case) to see if it is attached with screws or with clusters of spring fingers, like ours. The reinforcing cross member we removed in Step 1 makes a handy tool for prying free the facade.

Figure 7.19

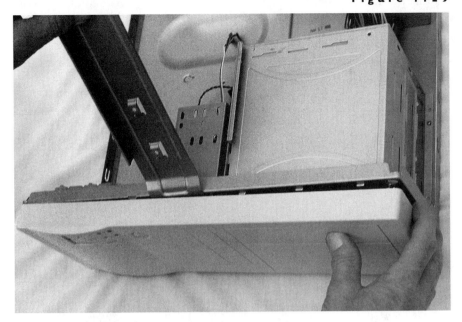

Removing the facade.

The drive cage is held in by two screws on the front of the case and a flat spring with a thumb release. You must remove the cage in order to put mounting screws in both sides of the drives. If you've ever worked on a PC from a really cut-rate computer shop, you'll see that they don't bother, and drives are essentially hung from the two screws on the top. Improper mounting can cause excess vibration in the drives and lead to long-term damage.

Figure 7.20

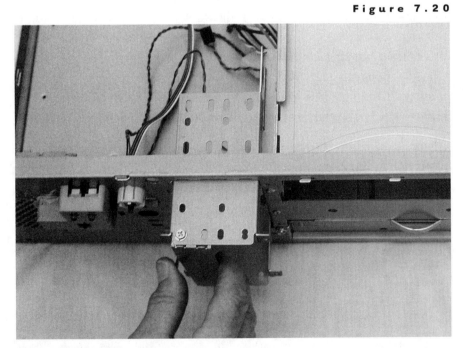

Removing the drive cage.

In this particular cage, it's easiest to mount the floppy drive first. The connectors on the drive must face the inside of the case. Line up the drive as far forward in the cage as you can, before loosely screwing in four fine screws (two per side). Make sure the drive is sitting all the way forward in the screw slots before tightening the screws.

Figure 7.21

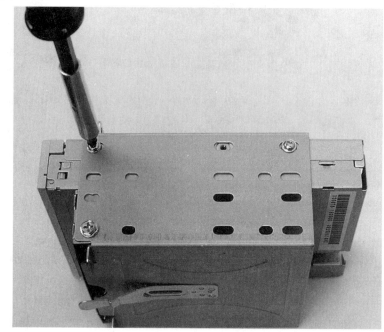

Screwing in the floppy.

The hard drive is mounted with four coarse-thread screws in the bottom of the cage. There is only one position in which the drive can be mounted in this cage, and it's a tight fit. We decided to put the hard drive and the CD drive on separate IDE controllers in this system, in part due to cable length considerations, in part for variety (our Pentium II/Celeron system was built with the standard master/slave arrangement). The drive selection jumper was left on the factory-installed position of "single."

Always preconnect the ribbon cable on the floppy drive before putting the cage back in the case (see Pentium II/Celeron Step 6 for more detail). On many desktop systems, the CD drive would be mounted with four fine screws at this point, before replacing the drive cage, which obstructs access to the inside screws. In this case, the CD drive is mounted with slide-in rails, so we can replace the cage before proceeding.

Figure 7.22

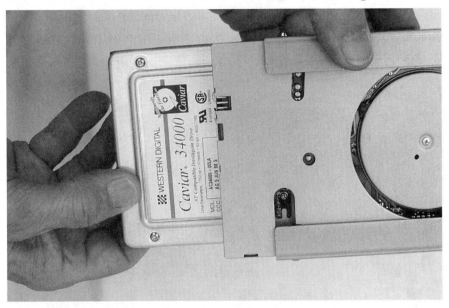

Putting the hard drive in the cage.

Replace the two screws in the drive cage immediately after you put it back in the case. The spring release that holds the cage in place is just a convenience; it does not offer any structural support.

Figure 7.23

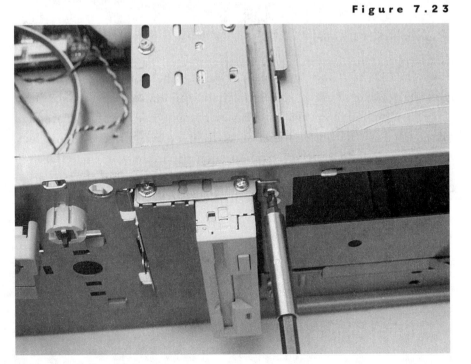

Screwing in the drive cage.

The rails are mounted on the bottom set of holes on the CD drive in our case (note the label is on top), but you need to check the alignment of the rails in your particular case. The rails are positioned with the screws all the way forward in the slots.

Figure 7.24

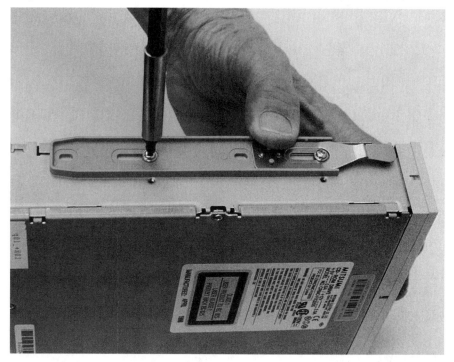

Mounting the CD railings.

Slide the CD drive into the case on its rails. If the drive seems to be dragging along the case frame, stop immediately and make sure that you have the rails mounted in the best positions possible. When the plastic faceplate of the CD drive is even with that of the floppy drive, the rails should lock into place. If the CD drive wants to slide in farther, you have the rails mounted too far back in the screw slots. Don't keep pushing the CD drive in to see where the rails lock or you'll be unable to get it out again without a great deal of effort.

Figure 7.25

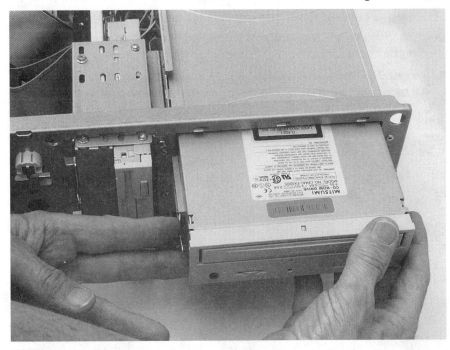

Sliding in the CD drive.

Since we decided to connect the hard drive and CD drive to different IDE controllers, the case will get a little crowded with ribbon cables. After you connect the power lead to the floppy drive, connect the ribbon cable to the hard drive. The red key wire on the ribbon cable is oriented toward the power connector on the hard drive.

Figure 7.26

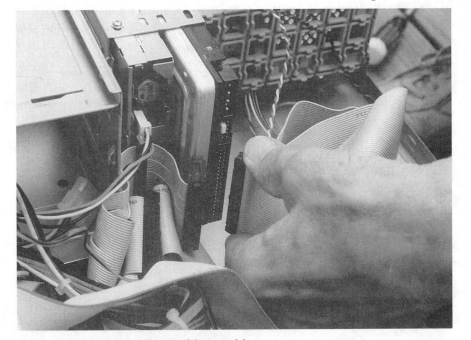

Connecting the hard drive ribbon cable.

Connect the power to the hard drive using the wide connector on the same lead used to connect the floppy drive. This isn't necessary from a power point of view, but it helps minimize the tangle of cables.

Figure 7.27

Connecting the hard drive power.

Connect the floppy ribbon cable to the motherboard, the CD drive ribbon cable to the secondary IDE port, and the hard drive ribbon cable to the primary IDE port. The ports are identified both in the motherboard booklet and on the motherboard itself. The "pin 1" location for all three ports is the same, so when you are finished, all of the red key wires on your ribbon cables should be oriented in the same direction.

Figure 7.28

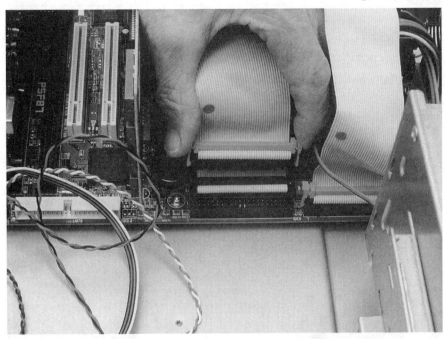

Connecting the ribbon cables to the motherboard (shown with cage removed for illustration).

The connections on the CD drive are exposed near the top of the case, where they are easy to read and connect. Use a fresh lead from the power supply to connect the power, and connect the audio patch cable. Connect the ribbon cable with the red key wire toward the "pin 1" end of the connector.

Snap the facade back over the front of case, and the drive installation is done.

Figure 7.29

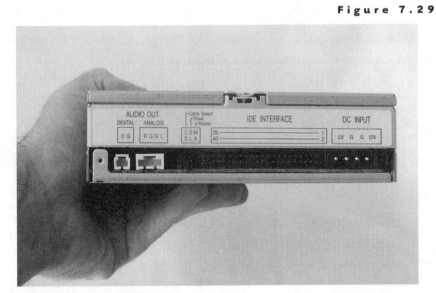

CD back (shown out of case).

Step 6. Installing Adapters

This system uses an inexpensive PCI video adapter that can be installed in any of the PCI slots. We chose to install it close to the I/O core for good spacing between adapters.

Figure 7.30

Installing a Trident PCI adapter.

Screw in the adapter immediately after installation. If you wait until you boot the system, you might give in to the temptation to put in the screw while the system is busy formatting the drive or loading the operating system. That can end in disaster!

We selected the standard Sound Blaster 16 PnP for our system. No jumpers needed to be set—out of the box and into the bus!

Figure 7.31

Installing Sound Blaster.

Immediately after screwing in the Sound Blaster, we install the audio feed from the CD drive. This allows the CD drive to play regular music CDs through your PC's speakers. Playing music CDs is a built-in function of CD drives. You can also listen to music through the headphone jack on the front of the drive after starting the player in Windows.

Figure 7.32

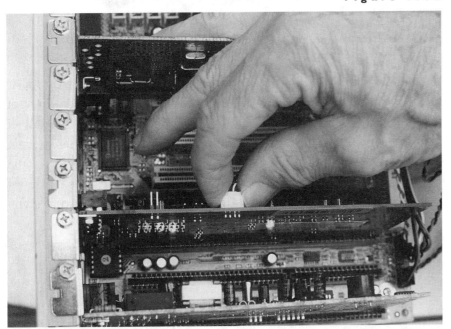

Connecting CD audio.

The modem we chose, a V.90- and X2-compatible 56-Kb/s modem, can be configured as Plug and Play or jumpered to a specific setting. We set the jumpers for COM1, interrupt 4, just to show it being done. The possible settings are given in a white matrix on the back of the adapter. We felt it was important to include an example of manually setting adapter resources in case your particular system has trouble configuring one of your adapters in Plug and Play mode.

Figure 7.33

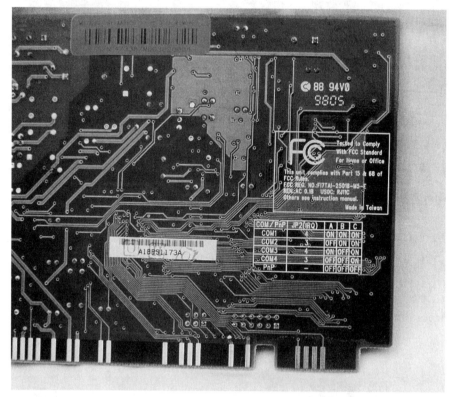

Jumper matrix on modem.

The jumpers we are talking about are located on the front of the card near the connector edge. The interrupt jumper (IRQ) is labeled on the front of the card also. When building a brand-new computer, you should install all of your adapters as Plug and Play, unless a problem arises. This modem could have been configured as Plug and Play by removing all of the jumpers, as per the jumper matrix. Never throw them away. You may need to manually force the modem to a particular COM port and interrupt if you add other adapters in the future.

Figure 7.34

Setting the modem jumper.

Screw in the modem, and that finishes the adapter installation. Notice that we left at least one empty slot between each adapter. This helps air circulation for cooling when using a full-height adapter, and makes the system easier to work on.

Figure 7.35

Screwing in the modem.

Step 7. Closing the Case

In Figure 7.36 we see the motherboard ports from the inside of the case, matched with the properly installed I/O shield. Note the circular group of holes directly over the I/O core, where an additional cooling fan can be installed. Although these fans are quite inexpensive, they just aren't necessary for most home PCs. For an example of installing an additional case fan, see our Athlon system in Chapter 5.

Figure 7.36

I/O core and additional fan opening.

It's now time to reinstall the structural cross member we removed in Step 1. Start by inserting the open-hinge end in the cage of the CD drive. Then lower the other end to lock into the slot, and screw it in place. After you put the screw in, pick up the whole case and give it a gentle shake from side to side to make sure there aren't any screws rolling around.

Note: Most PC builders will want to skip ahead to Step 8 at this point, connect the keyboard, power supply, and SVGA monitor, and turn on the PC to see if it lights up the screen. If it does, shut down, unplug the power supply, and proceed with replacing the cover. Software configuration and operating system installation should be done with the cover on.

Figure 7.37

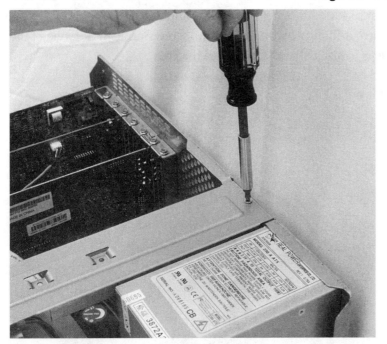

Securing the cross member.

The desktop cover, like the midtower cover, has channels formed of sheet metal that lock the sides of the cover to the bottom of the case. The cover should be placed on the case with 2 or 3 inches of overhang, at which point you can make sure that the sides are properly mated with the case frame. Slide the cover forward with two hands.

Figure 7.38

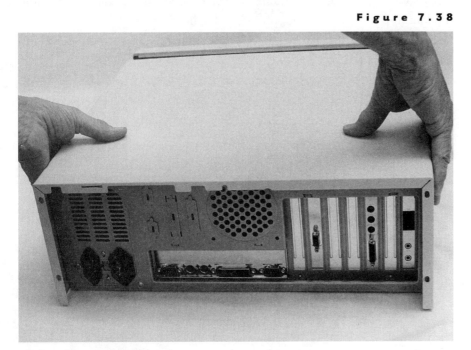

Sliding the cover forward.

Make sure that all of the cover edges are flush with the case before you begin replacing screws. The cover should seat easily as the screws go in. If you have difficulty getting any of the screws in the holes, one of the cover surfaces is probably not flush with the case.

F i g u r e   7 . 3 9

Securing the cover.

Starting at the left in Figure 7.40, the various connectors and ports are as follows: power cord, optional monitor power (not used), COM1, PS/2 mouse, PS/2 keyboard, parallel port (printer), COM2, SVGA port (for monitor), sound card (top to bottom—mike, line, speakers, game port), and modem (top to bottom—line, phone, mike, headset).

F i g u r e   7 . 4 0

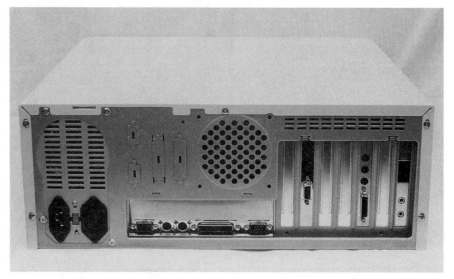

Fully assembled case back.

Step 8. Connecting Peripherals

We begin by connecting the keyboard, which goes in the right PS/2 port, as shown by the motherboard manual. The arrow on the connector is oriented directly up from the motherboard.

The mouse is connected to the other PS/2 port. Confusing the two leads won't cause any damage, but you would get a "keyboard failure error" if you tried to start the system.

Now we connect the power cord to the power supply and plug the free end into a wall socket. You will see a red switch immediately to the right of the power supply cord. In the United States, this should be set to 115 V.

Figure 7.41

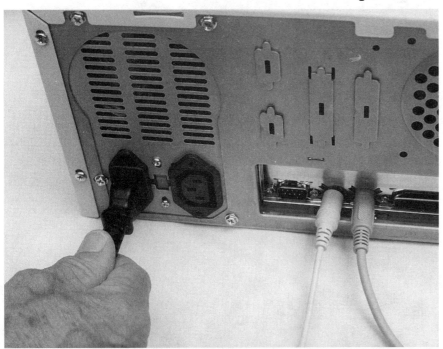

Connecting the power cord.

The modem port labeled "line" is connected to the phone jack on the wall using the phone cable that comes with the modem. If you have a telephone connected to the wall jack, you can reconnect it to the "phone" port on the modem. The telephone will work whether the computer is on or off, provided the line isn't in use.

Figure 7.42

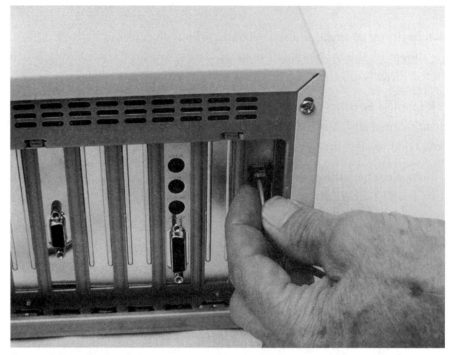

Connecting the modem.

The external speakers are connected to the sound card through the "speaker" jack (bottom of Figure 7.43). The connection is a normal mini-stereo plug, which has three contact areas: left channel, right channel, and ground. The "line" jack (top) is for connecting unamplified music sources,

Figure 7.43

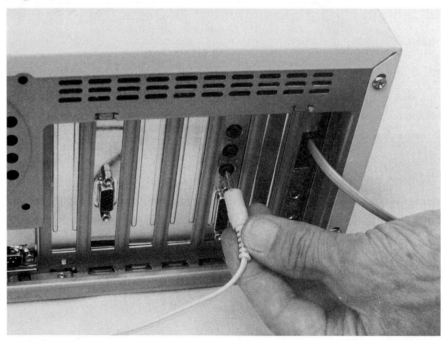

Connecting the speakers.

such as tape players, stereos, and musical instruments, to the sound card. This can be played through the speakers or converted into digital data and stored on the hard drive. The "mike" jack allows you to record your voice on the PC or to do speech recognition, where the PC actually transcribes what you say and responds to spoken commands. The 15-pin port at the bottom of the sound card is for attaching a joystick.

The monitor connector is a high-density, 15-pin D-shell, arranged in three rows. Be careful that you get the orientation correct (it will only go on one way) and that you don't try to force it on. The pins aren't very strong, and if you bend one by hurrying, it may break when you try to straighten it.

Figure 7.44

Connecting the monitor.

CHAPTER 8

Installing an Operating System

For the time being, the majority of PC builders will end up installing some version of Microsoft Windows on their PC. At press time, the choice was either Windows 98 or Windows 2000, and since Windows 2000 is both more recent and has a couple extra steps, we chose it for this chapter. Windows Millennium is due out before 2001 as a replacement for Windows 98, and at half the cost of Windows 2000, it will probably be the primary Windows operating system for the first part of the decade. Windows 2000 is really the replacement for Windows NT and is targeted at business users, not the home PC market. Linux is the up-and-coming alternative to Windows, and the number of applications that can be run on this "open source" operating system is exploding. "Open source" means that the actual code modules that make up the Linux operating system are available for modification by programmers, so the Linux community is constantly posting enhancements and compatibility fixes on the Internet for free download. There are also several branded versions of Linux that come with such extras like phone support and installation CDs, and we do a quick install of Red Hat Linux 6.1 in this chapter.

All modern motherboards are capable of booting from CD, that is, to load enough of an operating system so that the full install can proceed without needing to boot a floppy disk first. This is critical, because in years past, it was necessary to first prepare a floppy disk with the correct driver (i.e., software instructions) to allow the system to read the CD before the install could proceed. Among new motherboards, those that aren't quite so new may require you to enter CMOS, the same as if you were going to set the CPU speed, and under the "Advanced Setup" option, set the CD-ROM to the boot device. More recent motherboards simply scan all the drives for a bootable device when they power up, and the highly integrated motherboard used in the Pentium III build will look for a network boot drive if an operating system CD isn't found.

If the system has already finished searching for boot devices and is sitting there looking unhappy, you may have to hit the reset button once the CD is in. If you get a message like "CD boot failure" or "no boot devices found," but you know the correct CD is in the drive and you can see the drive LED light and hear the drive spin up, then you may have a minor timing problem. When the "try again" message appears (this may take many forms, such as "Hit F3 to try again," etc.), first eject and reinsert the CD. The drive will spin up automatically, and when this happens, go ahead and hit F3 or whatever button was required. This should ensure that the drive is ready when queried. If no option for trying again is offered, eject the CD tray, hit the PC's reset button, then reinsert the CD tray.

Installing Windows 2000 Professional

Windows operating systems of late all install about the same way. Power up the system and insert the operating system CD (not the Step by Step Interactive CD) in the CD or DVD drive. Unless you *are* trying to repair a problem, press Enter.

Figure 8.1

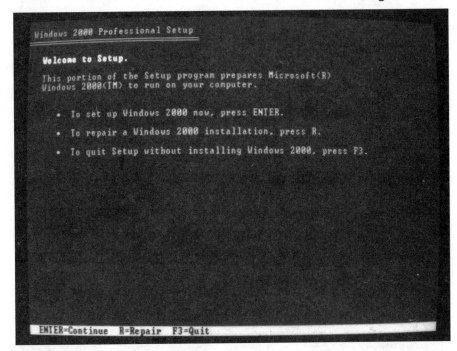

The Welcome to Setup Screen.

Microsoft now prompts you to accept their licensing agreement, euphemistically known as a EULA (End-User License Agreement). If you choose ESC for "I do not agree," the software politely dumps you out, and the installation does not proceed.

Figure 8.2

Windows 2000 Licensing Agreement.

Windows 2000 first looks around for where it will be installed. The Pentium III system onto which we loaded Windows 2000 was equipped with a 20-GB hard drive. Windows 2000 reports on the entire unpartitioned space (19.564 GB) and gives you the option of using all of it by pressing Enter, or some of it by manually creating a partition in the unpartitioned space.

Figure 8.3

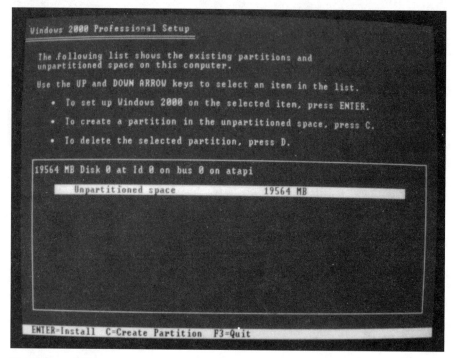

Partition options.

The next question relates to how the hard drive will be formatted. Generally speaking, the NTFS (NT file system) format is more flexible and reliable than the FAT (file allocation table) format, but third-party tools for after-the-fact disk management are more expensive. However, this is pretty much transparent to the user.

Figure 8.4

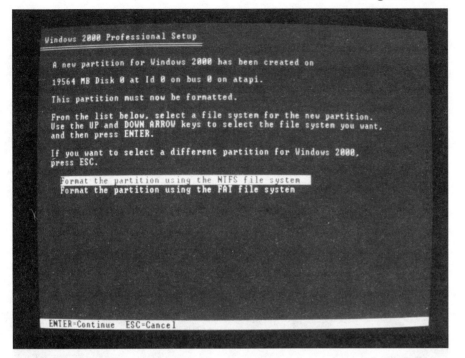

Format options.

Windows 2000 now proceeds to format your drive. This can take well over a half an hour on a drive as large as ours, though a progress bar is provided for your viewing enjoyment. Immediately after the format, Windows copies enough of itself to boot the system from the hard drive

Figure 8.5

Starting up.

over, and this can also be quite a yawn, even with the progress bar. Finally, Windows restarts the computer and boots from the hard drive. If you had an older system and you needed to make the CD-ROM the first boot choice to get the system to boot, you may need to change it back to C: (or IDE 0) at this point.

Next, Windows detects and installs all of your hardware. Ideally, this goes without a hitch, but that doesn't mean all the correct drivers for your hardware are actually installed. You should still install the CD that ships with your motherboard and any additional driver CDs that came with a video adapter or other parts once the operating system installation is completed and you can access the drive. When this step is finished, Windows presents you with your first real option, essentially asking whether you want to use U.S. defaults for the keyboard and units. From here on, you mainly hit Next a lot.

Figure 8.6

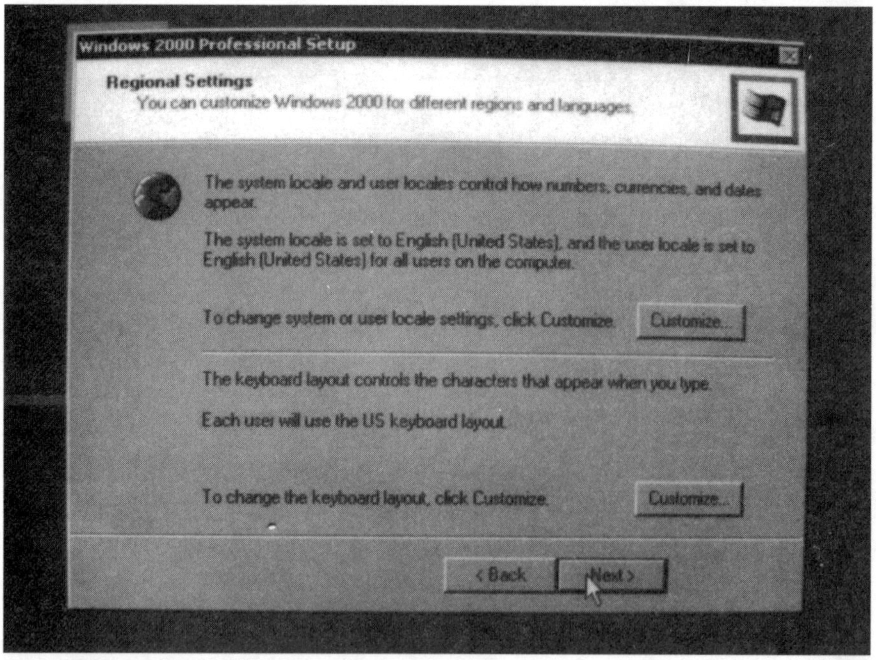

Regional settings.

Now comes your name and organization. This actually is used in some identification instances, but it's not visible to other people you may share a computer network with.

Figure 8.7

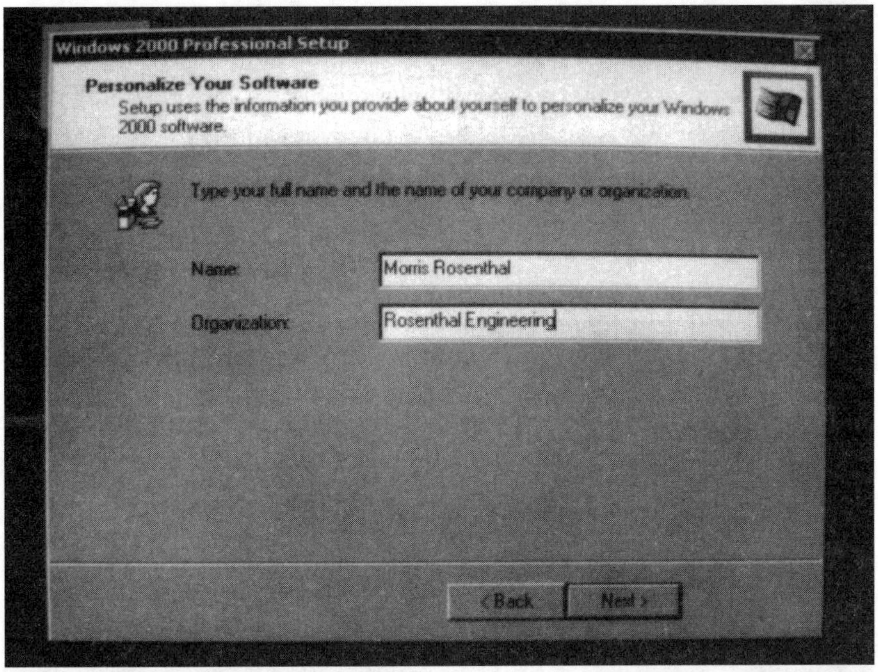

Personalize Your Software screen.

Next comes the encryption test (just kidding). Here you need to enter the product key that came with your Windows CD. Without it, the operating system installation aborts.

Figure 8.8

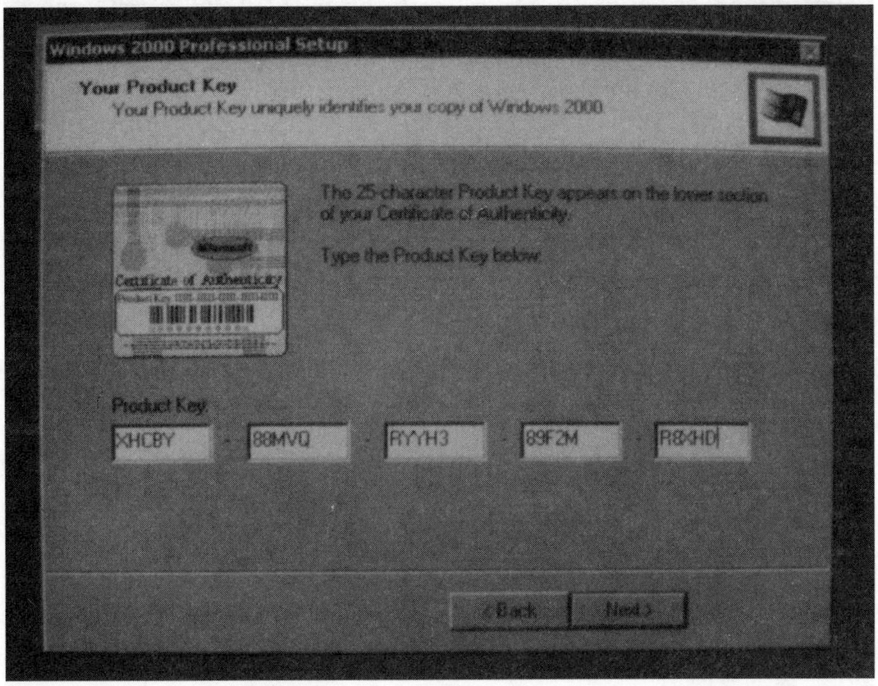

Entering the product key.

The computer name entered here is really the name your computer will show up as on Windows networks. For home use, I find the easiest way to avoid forgotten password problems is to enter no administrator password at all. The drawback is that a savvy burglar might take advantage and make up a password while breaking into my home, preventing me from accessing my own computer. Actually, those with children or spouses would be wise to enter something here.

Figure 8.9

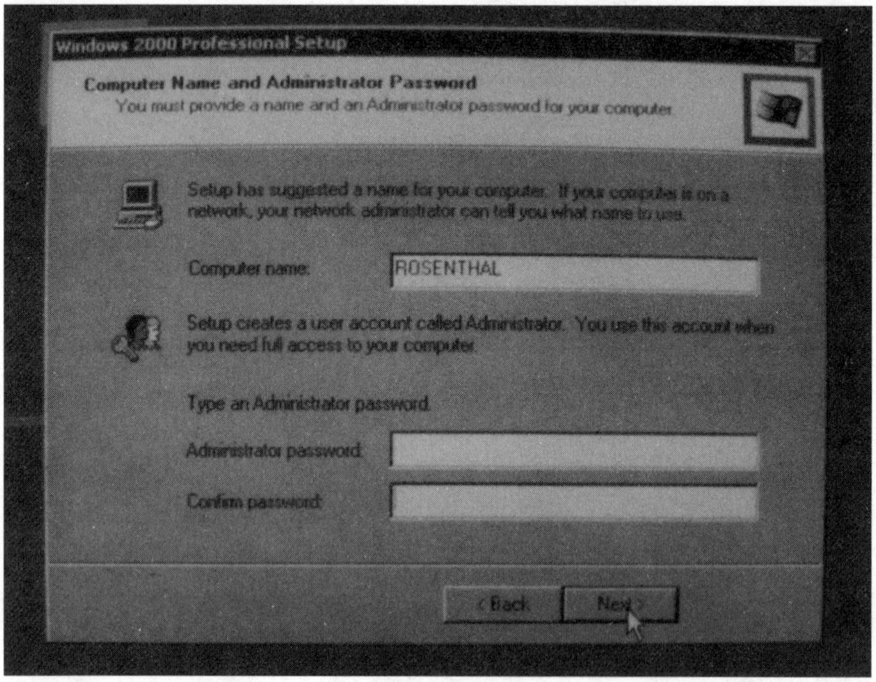

Screen for entering computer name and administration password.

Windows now retrieves the date and time from the PC's CMOS memory. The date and time can be set directly in the Standard Setup portion of CMOS, but it's just as easy waiting for the operating system to do it. You do need to select your time zone, and finding it quickly in the pull-down menu presents a geography test.

Figure 8.10

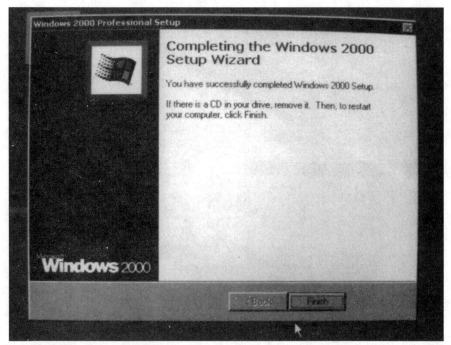

The Date and Time Settings screen.

Windows 2000 now performs some "final tasks," such as installing menu items, registering components, saving settings, and removing temporary items. An exciting progress bar accompanies this automated process. Finally it arrive at the end of the Setup Wizard, where clicking "finish" is the only option.

Figure 8.11

Completing Setup Wizard.

One good wizard leads to another, and the Network Identification Wizard appears. This step can be skipped if you aren't going to be connected to a Windows network.

Figure 8.12

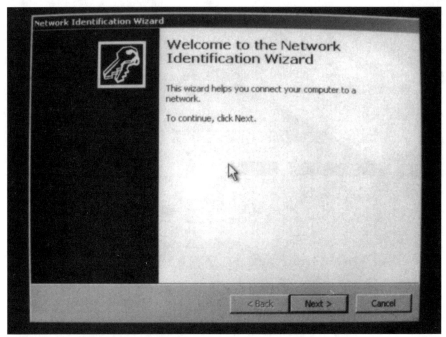

Network Identification Wizard.

Although the computer name is fixed, multiple users of the same computer are allowed. These users can be assigned different security privileges and access areas. Again, use of passwords can be bypassed by leaving those entries blank.

Figure 8.13

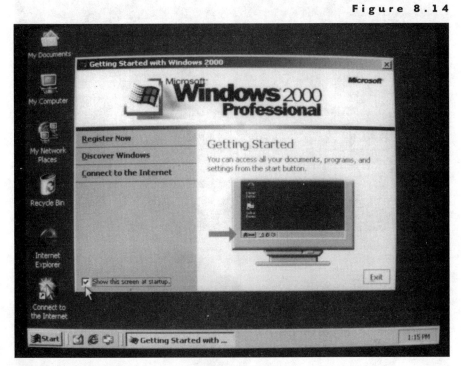

The Users of this Computer screen.

Another wizard completion screen now appears, although in addition to Finish, this one allow Back as an option. After hitting Next, the Windows 2000 Professional splash screen appears, shown in Figure 8.14. Until you uncheck the little box in the lower left-hand corner of the splash screen, it

Figure 8.14

Windows 2000 professional splash screen.

will continue appearing every time you start up the computer. Unless you want to register, explore the Discover Windows feature, or connect to the Internet (and you can do this at any time through a big item on the standard screen), uncheck the box, click Exit in the bottom right corner of the splash screen, and go to town!

Installing Red Hat Linux 6.1

This release of Linux comes on a bootable CD, just like the Windows operating systems. Upon starting the system with a new hard drive and the boot CD inserted, the Linux screen shown in Figure 8.15 appears. Beginners select the graphical mode install by hitting Enter. The next choice, that of language selection, shown in Figure 8.16, should be self-apparent.

Figure 8.15

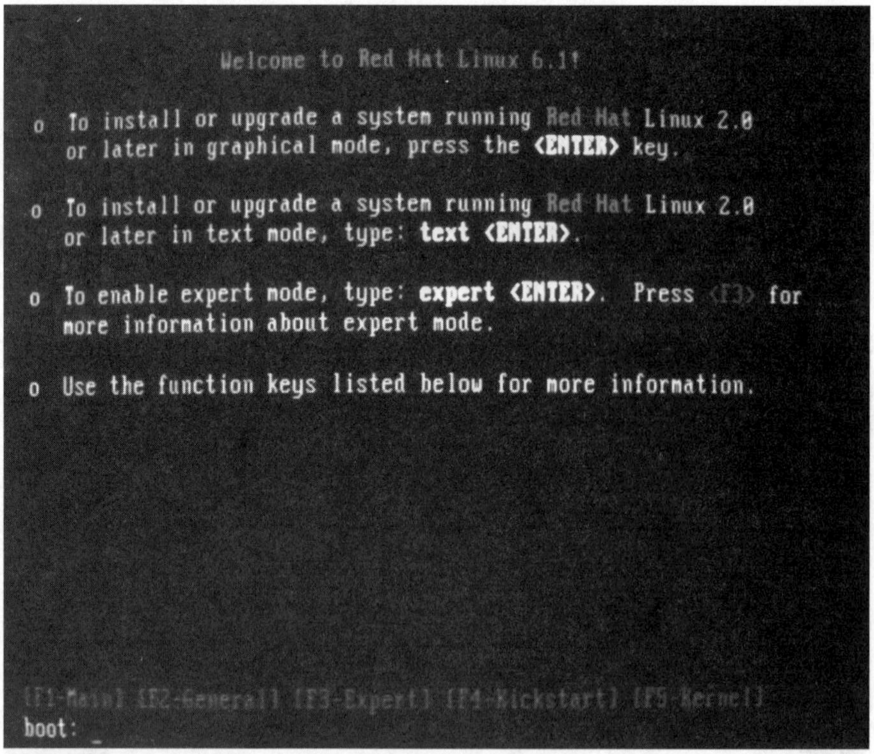

Red Hat Linux Install menu.

Figure 8.16

The Language Selection screen.

Now Linux runs us through a series of hardware input device selections, starting with keyboard type. Following the keyboard screen is a similar mouse configuration screen.

Figure 8.17

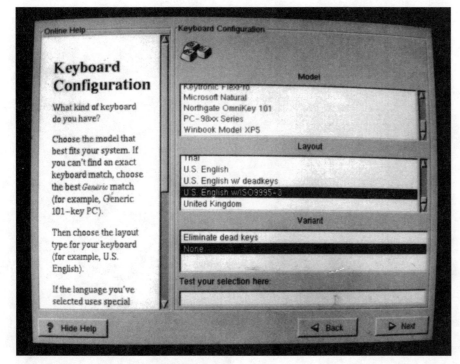

The Keyboard Configuration screen.

Not to be outdone by Microsoft, Red Hat has its share of screens that don't really require any user input, such as the "Welcome" screen shown in Figure 8.18. Hit Next.

Figure 8.18

The Welcome to Red Hat Linux screen.

There are three different install types you can do, plus custom and upgrade options. The most useful install for a new Linux user who just wants to fool around and learn about this operating system is a GNOME Workstation.

Figure 8.19

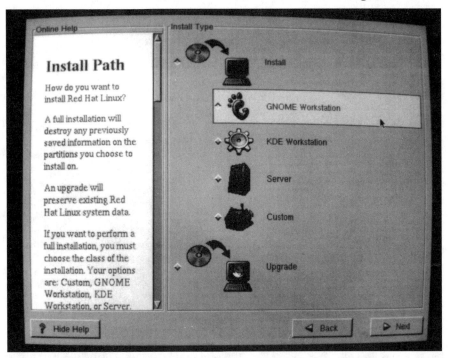

Choosing the installation type.

This distribution of Linux does include a transparent partitioning and formatting option. If you are installing Linux on a shared hard drive, you'll need to do a manual partition, *and read the instructions*. We simply go

Figure 8.20

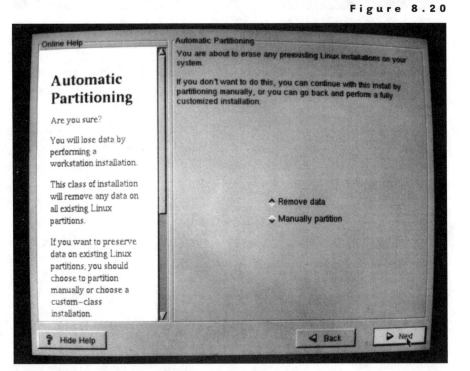

Partitioning and formatting.

with Remove Data, which has the effect of wiping out anything on the hard drive and installing Linux as the sole operating system.

Network configuration is required only if your Internet connection will be via an installed network card. If your Internet connection will be via modem, just hit Next.

Figure 8.21

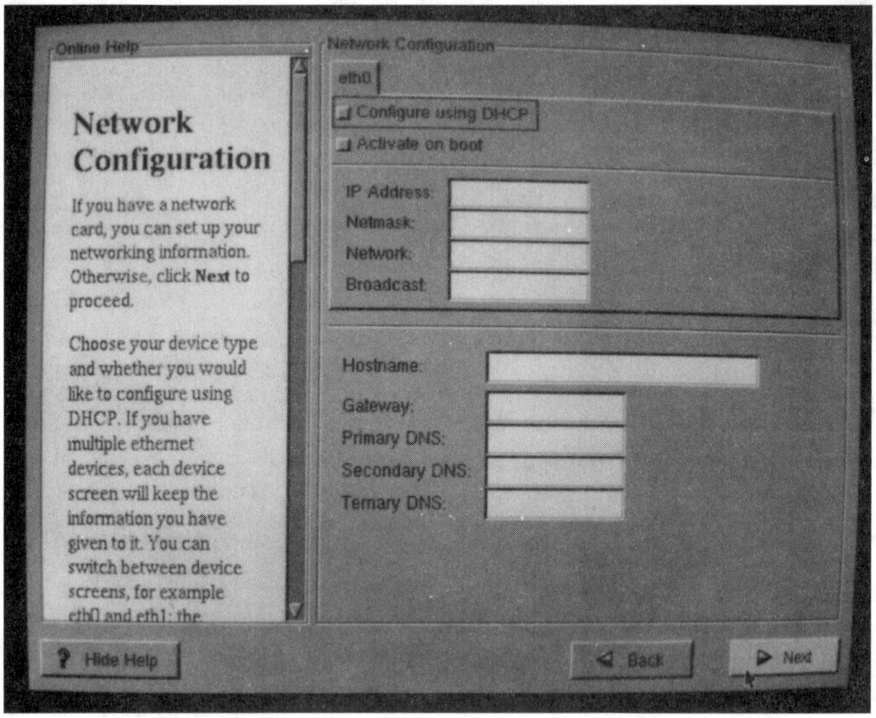

The Network Configuration screen.

Time zone selection is automatic, provided your systems date and time are correctly set in CMOS. Otherwise, you can switch to "Location" and override the selection.

Figure 8.22

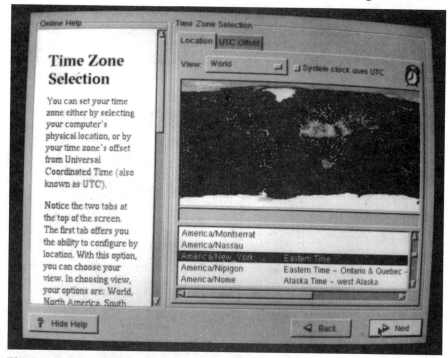

The Time Zone Selection screen.

You must create at least one user account in addition to a root password; doing so provides the highest level of access to the operating system. After this, Red Hat presents the graphical configuration screen, on which you choose your monitor type or a close competitor.

Figure 8.23

The Account Configuration screen.

The About to Install screen follows, which calls for a simple Click Next. Now Linux is actually installed on the hard drive, and you can see that the GNOME install takes 562 MB of space. The dual progress bar scheme is the envy of the operating system installer world.

Figure 8.24

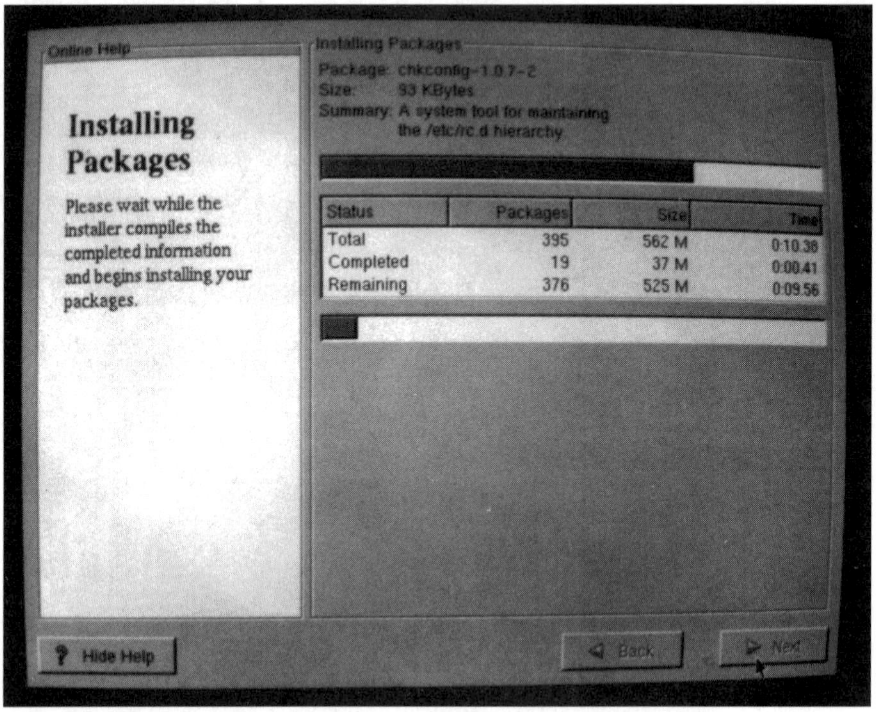

The Installing Packages screen.

Finally, Red Hat congratulates you on having installed Linux and adds, "Information on configuring your system is available in the post install chapter of the Official Red Hat Linux Users Guide." Linux is not yet quite as simple to completely set up and use as the consumer Windows packages, but most people tend to discount the time they've invested in learning Windows over the years. Give it a shot.

AGP (Accelerated Graphics Port)

This single adapter slot allows installation of a video adapter that can access the main memory of the system, improving both speed and efficiency. The single slot under the round battery in the center of the photo is the AGP slot.

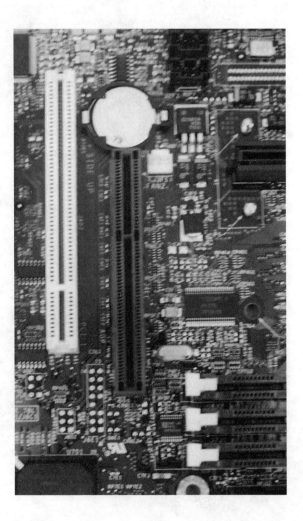

ATX

The AT eXtension is a new standard for motherboard, case, and power supply that makes building new PCs easier and more efficient. Features of ATX motherboards include the placement of the CPU next to the power supply fan for better cooling and the inclusion of all the standard I/O connectors on the motherboard.

CD drives

CD drives are an integral part of the modern PC. They have replaced the floppy drive as the primary means of loading software into the PC. CD recorders that can record on special blanks are becoming less expensive and more common.

Desktop case

The desktop-style case sits about 6 inches high, and takes up a couple square feet of desk space. However, the monitor can be placed on top of the case. Most desktop cases lack a removable motherboard pan, which is the outstanding feature of tower-style cases.

DIMM (Dual Inline Memory Module)

This type of memory has replaced SIMM (single inline memory module) memory in the newest PCs. A DIMM can serve up 64 bits of memory at a shot and is available in capacities up to 256 MB. Two 128-MB DIMMs are shown in the photo.

Drive cage

A removable sheet metal structure that holds drives, normally the floppy drive and one or more hard drives, in any type of case.

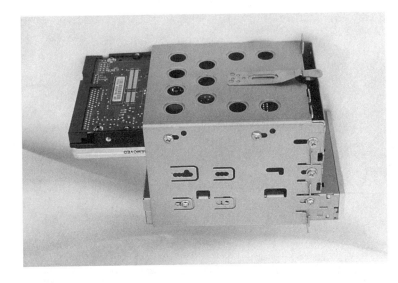

Floppy drives

These are still included in all new PCs. The 1.44-MB drive is the standard, using cheap magnetic discs to store copies of important data or to load small software applications or updates into your PC.

Hard drive

The hard drive is the primary storage system in the computer. Hard drives utilize rigid discs with magnetic coatings spinning at high speeds in a sealed enclosure to store and retrieve gigabytes of information with high speed and reliability.

Heat sink

All CPUs require active heat sinks for drawing away the heat generated in the small space of the microprocessor. Shown is a dual-fan heat sink for the AMD Athlon.

I/O Core

The I/O core consists of connection ports for features built into the ATX motherboard. The core is exposed through a standard opening in the ATX case, which must be fitted with an I/O shield designed for the particular motherboard.

ISA (Industry Standard Architecture)

All new motherboard are still equipped with a couple of old-style 16-bit ISA slots for installing slower adapters. Examples of brand-new adapters that get by fine with the performance of the ISA bus are modems and sound cards.

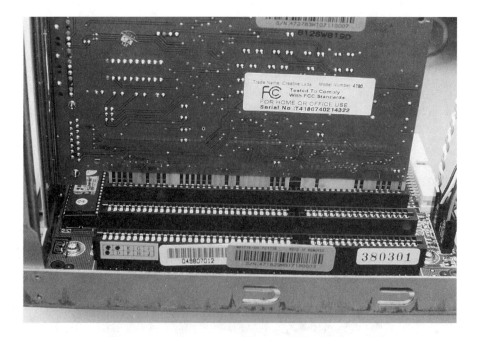

Keyboard (PS/2 style)

All new PCs use a PS/2-style connector with a 104/105-key keyboard. The keyboard connects directly to a PS/2 port mounted on the ATX motherboard. The keyboard shown includes extra Web navigation keys.

Midtower cases

These are nearly identical to minitower cases, just a little taller. Building PCs in tower-style cases is a little easier than in desktop cases, due to better access to drives and the removable motherboard pan of the tower design.

Modem

The modem allows the PC to communicate with the outside world over standard phone lines. The current technology allows speeds up to 56 Kb/s for downloading information from the Internet and the World Wide Web.

Monitor

Computer monitors, or screens, come in a huge range of sizes, capabilities, and prices. One advantage of larger monitors is the ability to display two pages side by side.

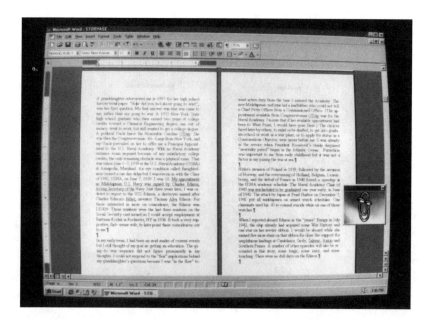

Motherboard (with pan)

The motherboard is the largest circuit board in the PC. It directly houses the CPU, memory, and all of the adapters. The motherboard is shown here mounted on a removable pan from a tower-style case.

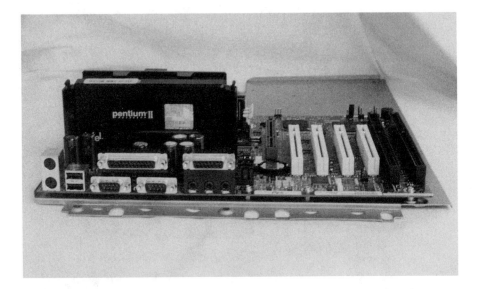

Mouse (PS/2 style)

New ATX PCs all provide a motherboard connection for the mouse, freeing up a serial port. The mouse is used to move a screen pointer and make selections.

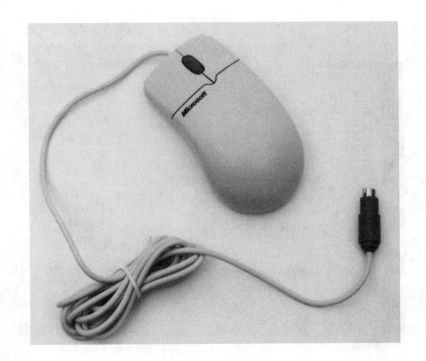

Network

Computer networks tie together large numbers of PCs. The most common technology currently in use in the office environment is 10BaseT, twisted-pair networking. A 10/100BaseT adapter is shown.

PCI (Peripheral Component Interconnect)

The standard high-speed bus in new PCs. A PCI card being inserted into a PCI slot is shown.

Power Supply

The ATX standard power supply support is controlled by a low-voltage signal switched by the motherboard logic. ATX power supplies are never completely off unless unplugged from the wall. They also provide several 3.3-V signals, used by the new motherboards.

Ribbon Cable

Ribbon cables are wide, flat cables formed from a large number of wires sealed side by side in a thin plastic coating. Shown are a floppy ribbon cable (narrow) and an IDE ribbon cable (wide).

SIMM (Single Inline Memory Module)

SIMM memory has been largely replaced by DIMM memory, but the newer SIMM modules are still supported by some of the new ATX motherboards. Shown in the photo are a new DIMM (64-bit) and an old SIMM (32-bit).

Slot 1

Slot 1 is the Intel replacement for Socket 7. The Pentium III, II, and Celeron processors are available as Slot 1 SECs (single-edge cartridges). The Slot 1 processor retention mechanism holds the CPU on the slot 1 motherboard.

Slot A

Slot A is the newest introduction to the PC world and is used exclusively with the AMD Athlon. Slot A and Slot 1 CPUs are similar in appearance but mutually incompatible.

Socket 370

Socket 370 is the newest CPU package from Intel. The Pentium III and the Celeron are both available in a Socket 370 version. Pictured is a Socket 370 Celeron.

Socket 7

The interface used for current AMD and Cyrix CPUs. Socket 7 CPUs are square packages with hundreds of gold-plated legs that are locked into the socket with a lever mechanism.

Video Adapter

The video adapter translates the computer-generated images into video signals that control the display on the monitor. An AGP video adapter is pictured.

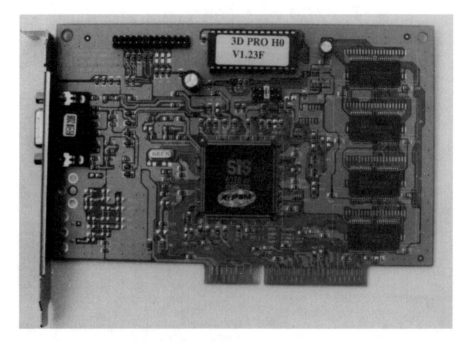

index

Note: Boldface numbers indicate illustrations; italic t indicates a table.

MORRIS ROSENTHAL is a writer and computer consultant. He has built or repaired hundreds of PCs and has trained numerous technicians. He has been featured on Dateline and in the national press as an expert on computer repair and purchasing issues. He is also the author of *The Hand-Me-Down PC*.